PLANTERS

PLANTERS

Make Your Own Containers
for Indoor and Outdoor Plants

by JACK KRAMER

BALLANTINE BOOKS · NEW YORK

Drawing Credits

Drawing numbers 1 through 18, and 27 through 30, are by Adrián Martínez. Drawing numbers 19 through 26, and 31 through 34, are by Robert Johnson.

Library of Congress Catalog Card Number: 76–56426
ISBN 0-345-25534-8-395

Manufactured in the United States of America
First Edition: March 1977

Contents

Also by Jack Kramer

*Beyond the House Plant: How to Create a Garden from Your Thriving
    House Plants In—and Out Of—Doors
The Complete Book of Terrarium Gardening
*Easy Plants for Difficult Places
Ferns and Palms for Interior Decoration
Garden Planning for the Small Property
Gardening Without Stress or Strain
*Grow Your Own Plants
*How to Identify and Care for Houseplants
The Indoor Gardener's First Aid Book
Indoor Gardening Without Soil: Flowers, Vegetables and House Plants
Indoor Trees
One Thousand Beautiful Garden Plants and How to Grow Them
One Thousand Beautiful House Plants and How to Grow Them
Orchids: Flowers of Romance and Mystery
Plants Under Lights
A Seasonal Guide to Indoor Gardening
*Starting from Seed
The Sun-Heated Indoor-Outdoor Room
The Underground Gardener
Underwater Gardens
Your City Garden
Your First Garden
Your Homemade Greenhouse and How to Build It

*Available in Ballantine Books editions, at your local bookstore.

PLANTERS

1. You Can Tell a Plant by Its Cover

If you are tired of conventional terra-cotta plant containers, or of paying high prices for them, it is time you looked elsewhere for exciting containers to dress up your plants. The terra-cotta clay pot is popular, but it is a clay pot—nothing more. There are hundreds of other possibilities—especially the decorative and distinctive containers you make yourself, which always have an appealing, "custom" look.

If nature is your thing, a coconut shell or a gourd makes a piggyback plant look unique; and a pretty seashell emphasizes the attractiveness of a peperomia. Boxes and planters complement the striking beauty of large plants like dracaenas and palms and enhance your home's or patio's decor. Hanging-basket containers set off ferns; terrariums show off the special delights of miniature plants. Coffee cans, inexpensive tile flues and concrete blocks, tubs, and jars and jugs are perfect for a host of indoor or outdoor plants: put some leafy seedlings in a coffee can; set large-foliage plants in a tile flue; fill a washtub with cascading petunias; try a cutoff jar or jug for philodendrons and pileas. You can even turn ordinary kitchen items like pots, pans, or pitchers into stunning accents with plants; and you can, for less or no expense, use salvaged items—your own or others'.

All of the above items—and more—can by some simple modifications be made plant containers that are handsome and distinctive, never ordinary or commonplace. And the best thing is that you not only will dress up your plants but will lessen the burden on your pocketbook.

If you are handy with tools, or not so handy (but have this book), make your own containers from wood. We include dozens of working drawings for boxes and tubs of all types and designs, for both indoors and out. You can let your imagination go wild and save acres of money doing it, *and* get what you want and not just what is available at suppliers'. Furthermore, the homemade is always more handsome (not to mention better-built) than the commercial.

When you make your own containers, you will be working with all sorts of materials in addition to wood: glass, acrylic, wire, wicker, and salvaged

Note the beauty of the wood in this homemade container; essentially a square box, the vertical bars provide character and charm. (Photo courtesy Western Wood Products.)

items. All these materials are easy to work with and require only a minimum amount of tools (hammers, saws, drills, glass cutters). As you work with these tools and materials, you will learn something about construction and perhaps move on to furniture-making as an extra bonus. In the following chapters, we will discuss each type of material and how to work with it.

The average commercially made 10-inch wood box costs $25 or more to buy. You can make it for $5. You can save money, too, by using salvaged coffee cans or drain pipes. Kitchen items such as salad baskets and jars are practically free, and a glass or acrylic terrarium can be made for as little as $5. If you are growing five or more plants *or* furnishing a patio with them, the savings from learning container craft will be substantial, and in the process you will come up with some unusual pieces you will be proud to display.

A simple hanging box container like this one can be made in minutes from seven pieces of wood. Total cost: $3. (Photo by Matthew Barr.)

But why bother to make your own containers when there is an overabundance of ready-made ones at nurseries and plant stores? (For that matter, why make your own preserves? Or clothes?) Aside from the obvious reasons of saving money, getting the containers you *want* (rather than what are available commercially), and owning strong, long-lasting containers, certainly not to be overlooked is the pleasure you will get out of container craftwork as an enjoyable and imaginative hobby—one which will give you the satisfaction of saying, "I made it myself."

Obviously a whole new world of fun is awaiting you if you venture into container crafts. We will show you all aspects of making "homes" for your plants, and the tour will be well worth it. Making your own containers will keep your mind going, your plants growing, and your bank account glowing.

Acrylic is elegant and serves well as a container for small houseplants. Working with acrylic is simple and requires little time and cost. (Photo by Matthew Barr.)

Rough construction-grade lumber was used for these outdoor planters. For a finished appearance, and to mask imperfections, wood trellises (or latticework) in a grid pattern were added. (Photo by Matthew Barr.)

A simple redwood hanging container can be made by almost anyone. (Photo by Matthew Barr.)

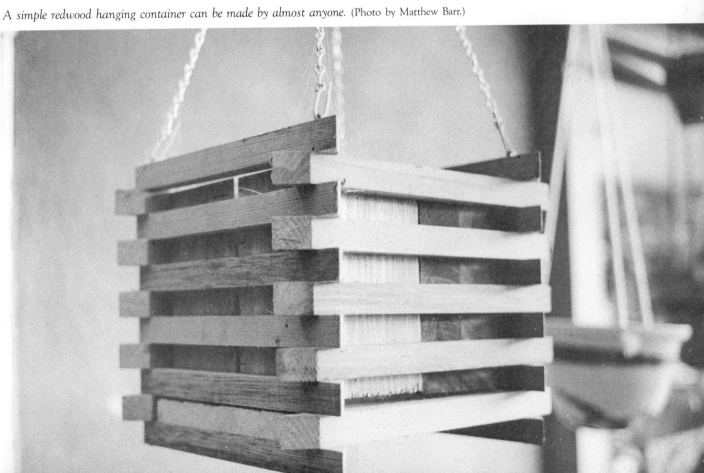

2. Wood Containers

Wood is the easiest material to use when making containers such as boxes and planters. (How to work with wood and what tools you need for woodworking are discussed in the next chapter.)

The wood container can be used indoors or outdoors. Indoors, boxes that have a finished appearance, such as those with moldings, are best. Drip saucers or trays will be necessary to catch excess water for any indoor container. These may be standard clay saucers, acrylic dishes, or even pie plates.

Boxes   A wood box for a plant may be elaborate in design or simple; it may have outside detailing or be perfectly plain. The plan of the box can vary too: it may have overlapped corners or crossed timbers, be spiral in shape or octagonal, and so forth.

Boxes for plants are popular, and easy and cheap to make. The box can be large or small, and square or rectangular or circular or part-circular—the size and shape depend on your imagination. The most simple box has four sides, and a bottom with drainage holes. What's more, you can merely nail a box together, but a combination of glue and screws makes a box last longer. Use brass screws and good-quality glue or epoxy. For small boxes, 1-inch lumber is fine; for large boxes, use 2-inch stock.

A standard 16 x 20-inch *rectangular* box is 5 inches deep and is made of redwood. It is suitable for annuals, bulbs, almost any small planting. Nail small chunks of wood under each bottom corner to elevate the box slightly. Another type of box, the *cube*, is neat and simple. For a 12-inch cube, use 1 x 12-inch strips of redwood. Screw and glue together the four sides and the bottom, and then—to give the box character—add some wooden 2 x 2-inch moldings (see Drawing 3 for an illustration of molding) at the top and edges. Run the edge moldings vertically, to define the box.

On boxes you can make other refinements, such as spacing the slats ½ inch apart, tacking trelliswork onto the face of the box, or, if you are highly imaginative, scoring the box with a simple design to give it dimension. You

Overlapped-Corners Container

Drawing 1

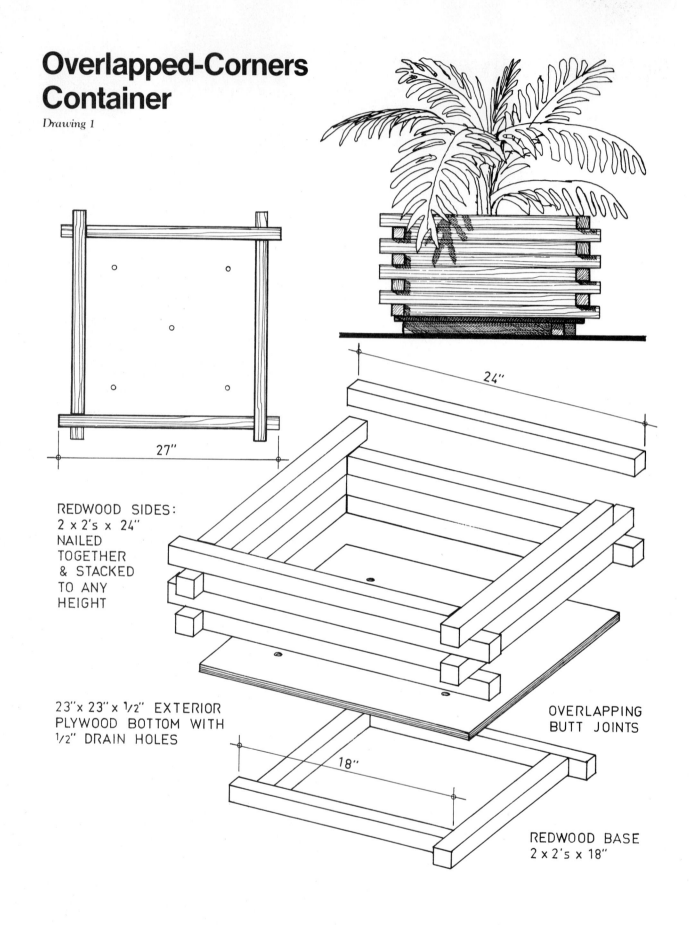

REDWOOD SIDES:
2 x 2's x 24"
NAILED
TOGETHER
& STACKED
TO ANY
HEIGHT

24"

27"

23" x 23" x ½" EXTERIOR
PLYWOOD BOTTOM WITH
½" DRAIN HOLES

OVERLAPPING
BUTT JOINTS

18"

REDWOOD BASE
2 x 2's x 18"

Spiral Container

Drawing 2

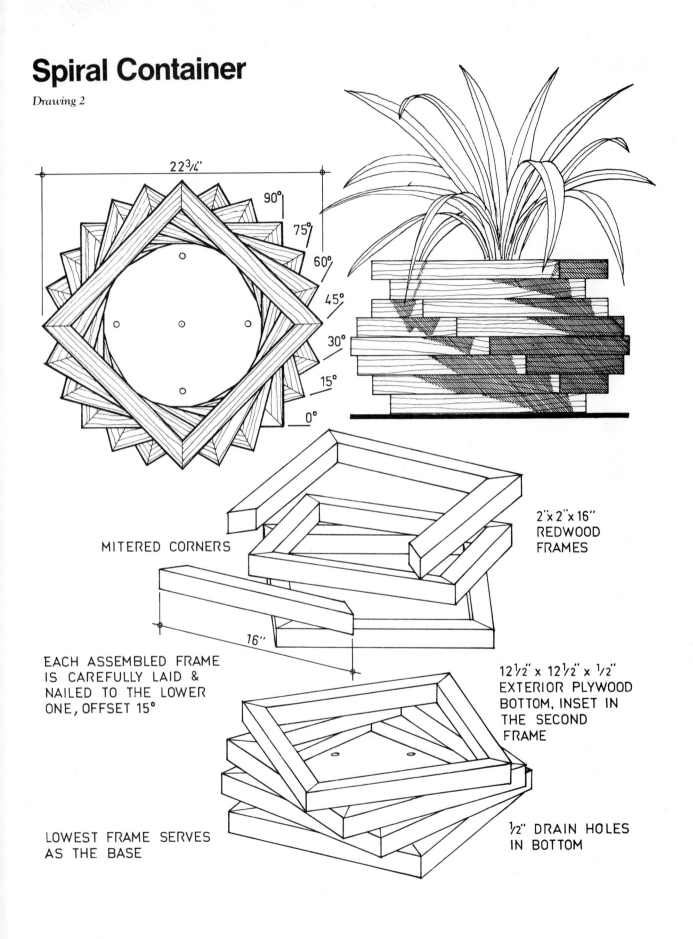

22³/₄"

90°
75°
60°
45°
30°
15°
0°

MITERED CORNERS

2"x 2" x 16"
REDWOOD
FRAMES

16"

EACH ASSEMBLED FRAME
IS CAREFULLY LAID &
NAILED TO THE LOWER
ONE, OFFSET 15°

12½" x 12½" x ½"
EXTERIOR PLYWOOD
BOTTOM, INSET IN
THE SECOND
FRAME

LOWEST FRAME SERVES
AS THE BASE

½" DRAIN HOLES
IN BOTTOM

Molding Details

Drawing 3

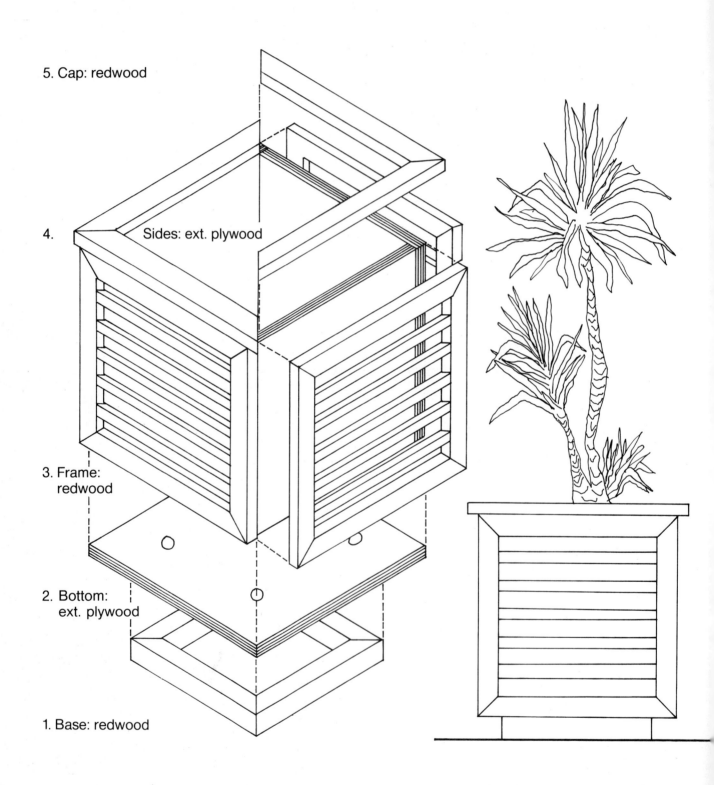

5. Cap: redwood

4.   Sides: ext. plywood

3. Frame:
   redwood

2. Bottom:
   ext. plywood

1. Base: redwood

can also taper the box and bevel (angle-cut) the corners and use a plywood base for a more finished appearance. As you will see from our drawings, there are innumerable ways to make a box *more* than a box.

Planters   Planters, contrasted with boxes, are wooden boxes that are longer and narrower (at least so is the prototype planter) or of window-box shape. The design of the planter needs some thought: small planters coordinate with small plants, large ones with big plants.

Planters can be used at floor or ground level, and indoors (built-in planters) or outdoors (on patios and decks). Outdoors, you *should* elevate your planters with 2-inch blocks under each corner so air can enter the box from underneath and thus eliminate hiding places for insects. In the home, planters *must* be raised for maximum good looks.

Indoors, the planter is basically used to define a long space: in a stairwell, along a window, or as a room divider. The indoor planter must be made from kiln-dried wood and should have a galvanized-metal insert and some drainage facilities. Have a sheet-metal shop make the insert, and have them put in a spigot.

A variety of wood containers, most of which can be made at home. When you make your own, you can choose from many designs. Note that many of the containers have a wood molding—which gives a finished look. (Photo by Matthew Barr.)

These are commercially made wood containers, at a nursery. You can make them yourself and save money. (Photo by Matthew Barr.)

For the best look, paint planters white or a neutral color. Also, design and motif are most important for indoor planters. The indoor planter is perhaps the most difficult container to make properly, because it needs careful craftsmanship and good finishing touches to be totally handsome in a room.

Outdoor planters are easy to make (usually just four sides and a bottom) and can be built from construction-grade redwood. They need not be painted, and if they are made of redwood they will eventually turn a lovely silver color. For finishing touches, use moldings or caps at their tops. Make outdoor planters from 2 x 4- or 1 x 12- or 2 x 12-inch lumber; a good size is 12 inches wide, 10 inches deep, and 36 inches long. (Of course you can alter this

Interior Demountable Unit

Drawing 4

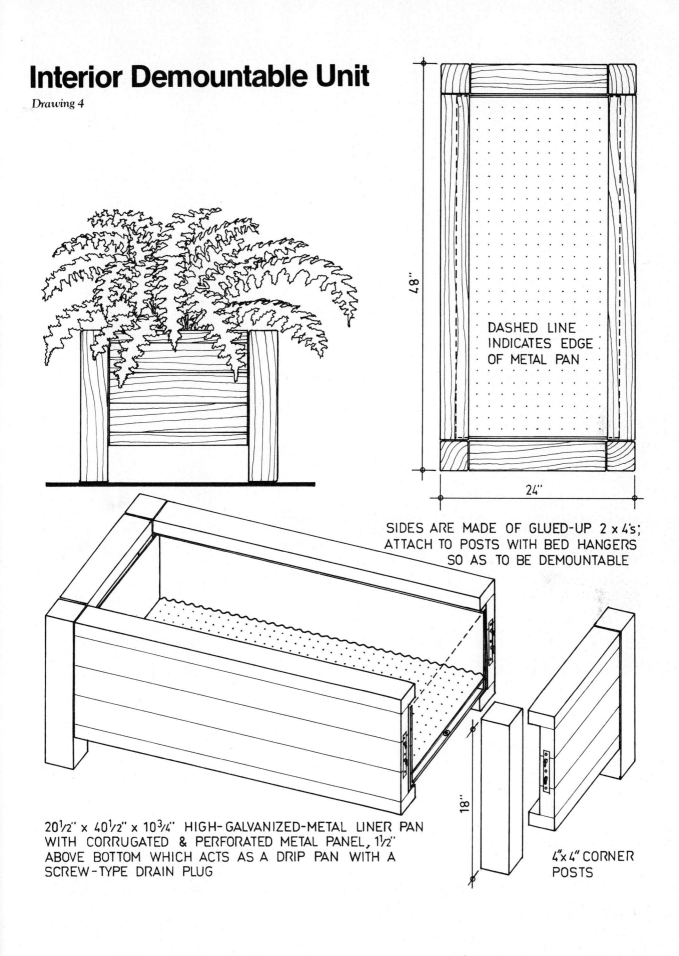

48"

24"

DASHED LINE
INDICATES EDGE
OF METAL PAN

SIDES ARE MADE OF GLUED-UP 2 x 4's;
ATTACH TO POSTS WITH BED HANGERS
SO AS TO BE DEMOUNTABLE

18"

4"x 4" CORNER
POSTS

20½" x 40½" x 10¾" HIGH-GALVANIZED-METAL LINER PAN
WITH CORRUGATED & PERFORATED METAL PANEL, 1½"
ABOVE BOTTOM WHICH ACTS AS A DRIP PAN WITH A
SCREW-TYPE DRAIN PLUG

size to your needs and the plants you want to grow.) Large plants will, by necessity, need large planters, though small plants can be accommodated in a 12- or 16-inch box.

Handsome square modular stacking planters can be used outdoors in varying plans to create a total container garden: stacked, lined up, and so forth. A practical size is 20 x 20 inches. Indoors, the modular planter does not look handsome, since it takes up too much space and for some reason seems incongruous with home furnishings.

Built-in Planters   The built-in planter was popular in the 1930's and is making a comeback. These planters are room dividers, stair railings, windowsills, racks, or accent "islands" near stairwells. Properly made and built with some imagination, built-in planters are very attractive, but made improperly and put in an unsuitable location they can be ugly.

The built-in planter always adds charm to a room; here it is used as a partial divider, and the total setting is pleasing. (Photo by Ken Molino.)

Built-in indoor planters require a good hand at carpentry and then excellent finishing work—painting, sanding, and so on. Such planters also need galvanized bin inserts for the plants, which can be costly. However, if you have little space for plants in your home, the built-in planter is the answer, because you can grow many plants in what may otherwise be unused space.

The interior windowsill planter is a terrific one to build; it looks good and works beautifully because it is near the window, thereby giving your plants sufficient light. The planter in a bookcase or as a room divider is not as successful, although if you use low-light-type plants they will probably survive in such uses.

Before you embark on a built-in planter, consider all the factors: Is there enough light for the plants? Will the material used match the existing woodwork? What will the total cost be?

An outdoor container—and a big one—this plant housing is made from 2 x 2 rough redwood neatly trimmed in trellis, or latticework, design. (Photo by Matthew Barr.)

Window Box

Drawing 5

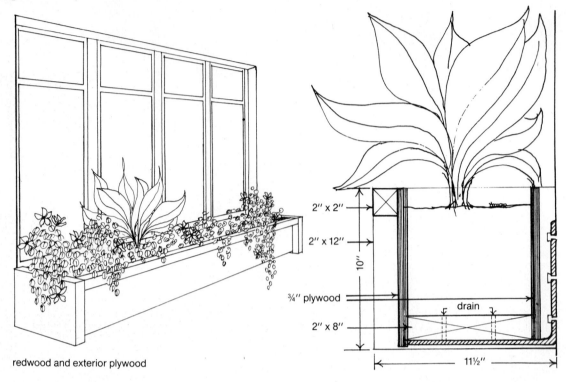

redwood and exterior plywood

2″ x 2″
2″ x 12″
10″
¾″ plywood
2″ x 8″
drain
11½″

Window Boxes   Window boxes (see Drawing 5) are popular in Europe, but here, unfortunately, they are not used as much as they could be. The window box is actually a very effective way of having some flowers or tiny vegetables even if you live in an apartment. The drawbacks are that in winter the box must be covered, and looks bleak. Also, a window box may not be permitted in an apartment building. But window-box greenery does a lot to make some gardening possible in the city, so check with your landlord if you are a cliff dweller.

Nurseries sell plastic or wood window boxes, but these are not esthetically handsome or, usually, of the right size. You are better off making your own window box. Use redwood or cedar, at least 1 inch thick, and a plywood (¾-inch) base. Regardless of the design you decide on, make the window box at least 10 inches wide and 10 inches deep, to allow enough root room for the plants. Drill drainage holes in the bottom of the box at about every 8 inches.

The window box can be a simple rectangle with straight sides; or, if you live in severe winter climates, consider a box that has a sloped-outward edge. This type of window box lets soil expand when it is frozen—without damaging the box.

Attaching the box to the window is more difficult than actually making the box. Use metal L-shaped brackets for support under the box; to really secure the box to the house wall, use screws, lag bolts, or toggle bolts.

Window boxes like these are available at nurseries—or make your own by using the design shown, opposite. (Photo by Matthew Barr.)

3. Working with Wood

Many of the handcrafted containers in this book are made from wood. Wood is easy to work with; you do not have to be a carpenter or be very handy with tools. In fact, if you don't want to do *any* cutting or sawing at home, you can order (for a slight cost) all wood pieces for the design you've made cut to size. Then all you have to do is nail, screw, or glue the parts together to make your boxes or planters or other containers. Also, you will be using mainly small pieces of wood for your plant containers rather than lumber ("lumber" denotes large boards), so you really have nothing to fear. Just make sure you have the proper tools and know something about adhesives and wood epoxies (we will give you information about tools and these materials later in this chapter).

Wood: What to Know About It

The basic wood for containers is either redwood or cedar, because these woods resist weathering. For outdoor use, construction-grade redwood— that is, redwood with a few slight defects—is fine. For indoor use, purchase *kiln-dried* redwood or cedar; this wood is blemish-free and smooth to the touch. Indoors and out you can also use pine or Douglas fir—if you protect the wood with preservatives or paint. (There are many preservative coating products at paint stores.)

If you do not want to cut the wood for your container at home, tell the lumber dealer the size boards or pieces you need and he will cut the wood for you. Order wood first by thickness, width, and length; for example, 2 inches x 6 inches x 8 feet long. Next, specify what type of wood you want, such as redwood; and then indicate the grade, such as construction-grade, kiln-dried, rough, and so on.

There are a few fundamentals about ordering wood which you should know, if you don't already. Bear in mind that if you order, say, standard 2 x 4-inch boards, the *actual* dimensions of the boards will be 1½ x 3½ or slightly larger. In other words, the boards will never be exactly 2 x 4. Also, remember that pieces of wood smaller than 2 x 4 inches are referred to as "strips." You would call these strips 2 x 3's or 1 x 2's, for example. Another reminder: posts for corner construction are either 4 inches or 2 inches square.

Detailing Containers

No matter what kind of wood container you are making, if the bare look of wood is not to your liking, you can easily alter it by various detailing methods.

With a little extra time and very little more money, wood containers can be handsomely detailed on the outside. You can use wood strips to form such outside designs as latticework and diamond patterns. The detailing puts the finishing touches on the containers and adds a note of elegance.

A simple but effective outside-the-container motif is a raised rectangle outlining the container, which creates a shadowbox effect. For the average container this requires sixteen pieces of 1 x 2-inch strips of wood. Another method is to place strips of wood vertically or horizontally ½ inch apart; this will add flair to the basic box—and cover any construction mistakes.

When you detail a wood container, you should always add a molding (or cap) at the top to give it finish and add dimension. Caps are usually 1 x 3 inches; nail them in place, letting the outer edge overhang the container by ½ to 1 inch.

The beauty of wood as a container material is shown in this handsome piece. The box was joined with heavy staples and wood epoxies rather than with the more conventional nails. (Photo by Matthew Barr.)

Plant Ladder

Drawing 6

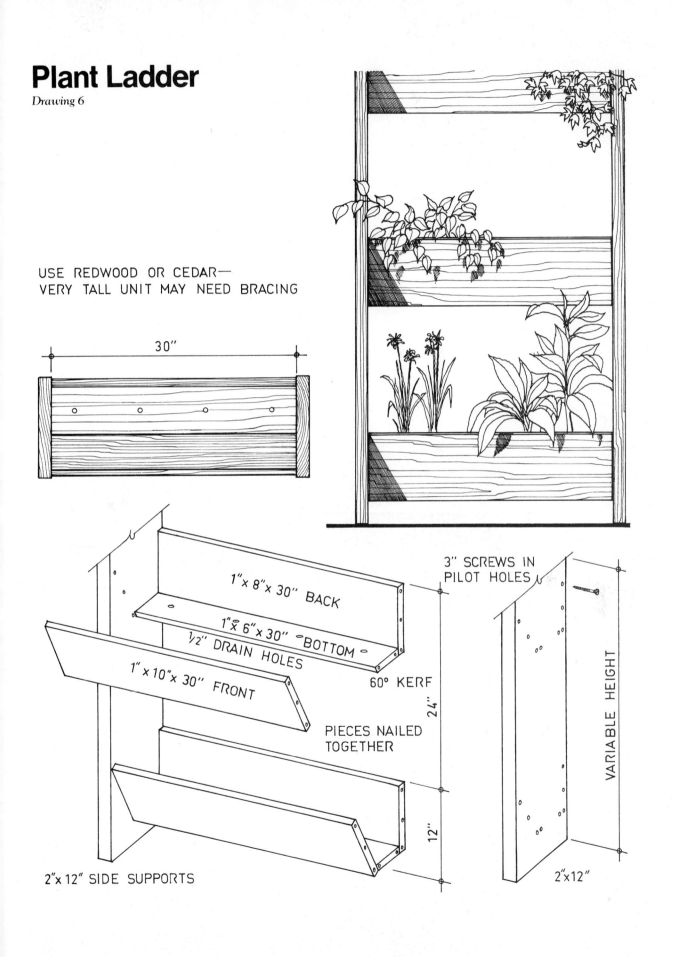

USE REDWOOD OR CEDAR—
VERY TALL UNIT MAY NEED BRACING

30"

1" x 8" x 30" BACK

1" x 6" x 30" BOTTOM

1/2" DRAIN HOLES

1" x 10" x 30" FRONT

60° KERF

PIECES NAILED
TOGETHER

3" SCREWS IN
PILOT HOLES

24"

12"

VARIABLE HEIGHT

2" x 12" SIDE SUPPORTS

2" x 12"

These wood containers have been sanded to emphasize the wood grain. The effect is lovely. (Photo by Matthew Barr.)

If you are handy with tools, you might want to score a container with a design. Use a wood chisel to create various patterns. A basic scoring pattern is a simple knife edge ¼-inch-deep, spaced ½ to 1 inch, vertically or horizontally, on the container. This design will add beauty to the container and create a bas-relief effect.

Sandblasting is another way to add a textured, handsome look to a container; you can rent a sanding machine. Or, if you are making a small container, sand the wood by hand to a lustrous, smooth finish.

Since the detailing of the outside of the container depends mainly on its size, proportion and symmetry should also be considered. For example, large containers can be detailed with big strips of wood; smaller containers need more meticulous detail and smaller pieces or strips of wood.

To enhance the appearance of this large box, grid-pattern scoring has been applied. (Photo by Matthew Barr.)

Coverings for Containers   A covering is a material applied to the exterior of the container to give it an elegant look. There are many dramatic coverings you can use.

For example, you can nail or glue thin sheets of silver, bronze, copper, or even gold to the wood, *or* attach the material with a molding. A container decorated with metal is especially striking indoors.

A leather-laced container is similarly attractive. Lace the leather at the corners of the container with a running stitch. Use upholstery needles and cord. To prevent the covering from getting moldy from excessive moisture, spray the *inside* of the container with silicone and then line it with a layer of clear plastic or aluminum foil.

A mirrored box, too, blends beautifully with many interiors. Sheets of mirror are sold at most hardware stores; or have mirroring cut to size at a

Square "Tubes"

Drawing 7

USE REDWOOD OR CEDAR

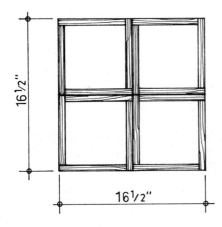

16½"

16½"

EACH UNIT IS ASSEMBLED
WITH GALVANIZED NAILS

THE FOUR UNITS ARE JOINED WITH
1¾" CADMIUM-PLATED BOLTS

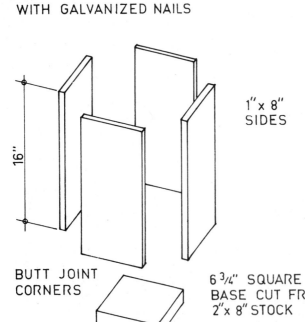

16"

1" x 8"
SIDES

BUTT JOINT
CORNERS

6¾" SQUARE
BASE CUT FROM
2" x 8" STOCK

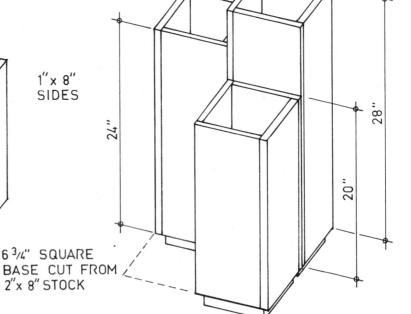

24"

20"

28"

glass shop. Ask for DSB (⅛-inch-thick mirror), and buy the proper adhesive at the store. Dab the adhesive onto the basic wood container, and merely set the mirrors in place. Tape the corners of the mirrors with masking tape to ensure the sealing. After twenty-four hours you can remove the tape.

Another unique covering, although somewhat harder to apply, is wire. The design can be either horizontal or vertical lines, spaced ½ to 1 inch apart on the container. Anchor the wire with small nails along both the top and bottom edges of the container; wind the wire around the nail on one edge, stretch it taut to the opposite nail, wind the wire in place around this second nail, and so on. You can use silver, bronze, or gold wire (whatever is available at your hardware store). String may also be used in place of wire, but it is not as handsome or as durable. The wire- or string-covered container is best for interior use, where some embellishment is usually necessary or desirable to suit the container to the decor.

This "container" is actually a fruit crate set on end, with some of the slats removed. A potted plant has been placed inside the crate. (Photo by Matthew Barr.)

Crossed-Timbers Container

Drawing 8

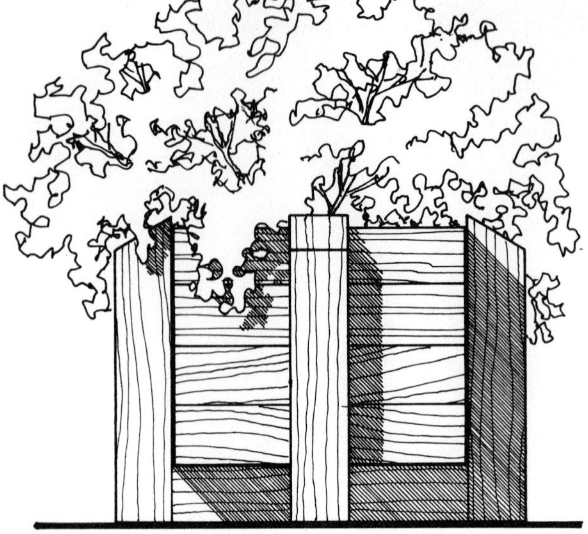

USE REDWOOD OR CEDAR

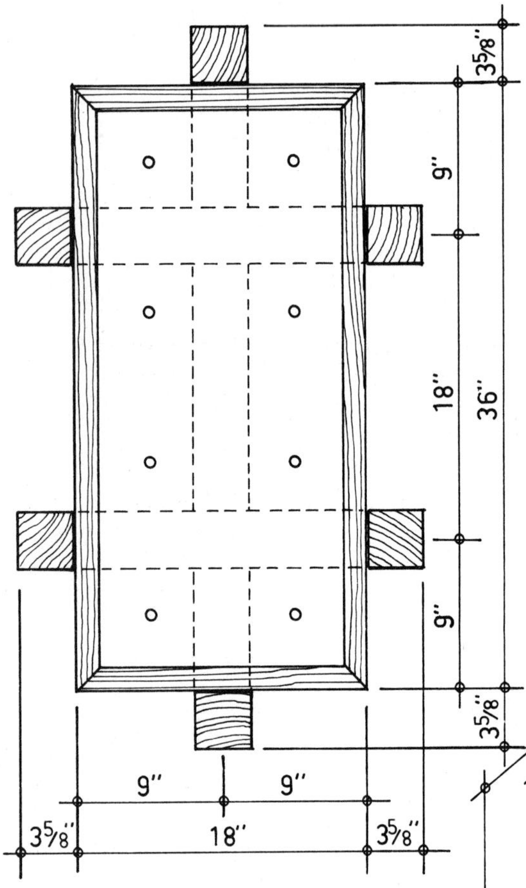

3⅝"

9"

18"   36"

9"

3⅝"

9"   9"

3⅝"   18"   3⅝"

2"x 4" SIDES, MITERED CORNERS

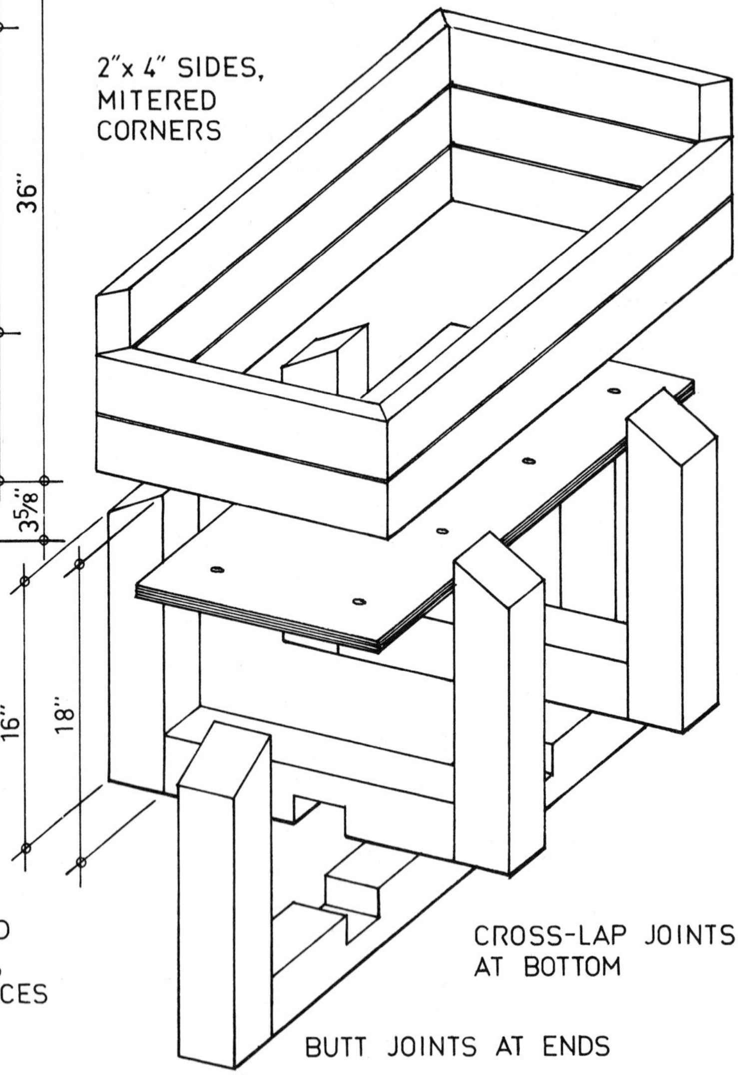

16"   18"

4"x 4" CROSS-SUPPORTS, 30° ANGLED TOPS

14¾" x 32¾" EXTERIOR PLYWOOD BOTTOM WITH ½" DRAIN HOLES, INSET BETWEEN 2"x 4" SIDE PIECES

CROSS-LAP JOINTS AT BOTTOM

BUTT JOINTS AT ENDS

Stepped-Timbers Container

Drawing 9

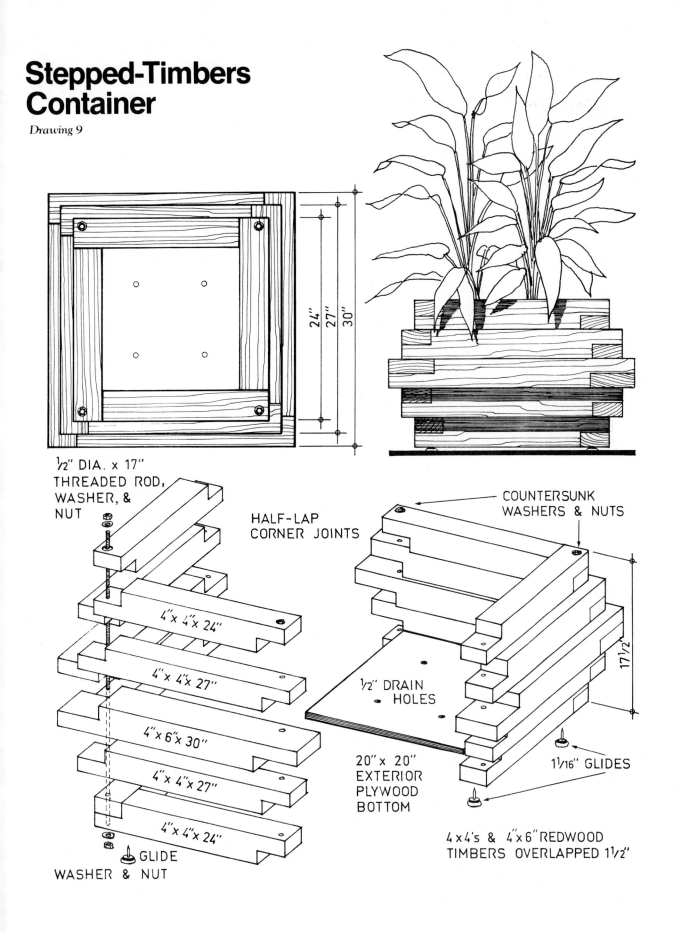

24"
27"
30"

½" DIA. x 17"
THREADED ROD,
WASHER, &
NUT

HALF-LAP
CORNER JOINTS

COUNTERSUNK
WASHERS & NUTS

4" x 4" x 24"

4" x 4" x 27"

4" x 6" x 30"

4" x 4" x 27"

4" x 4" x 24"

GLIDE

WASHER & NUT

½" DRAIN
HOLES

17½"

20" x 20"
EXTERIOR
PLYWOOD
BOTTOM

1 1/16" GLIDES

4 x 4's & 4"x 6" REDWOOD
TIMBERS OVERLAPPED 1½"

Tools   You do not need extensive tools to make wood containers. You will, however, need a good hammer. I prefer the claw hammer of forged, high-quality steel. Hammer faces, or heads, are flat or slightly convex; the convex hammer, which lets you drive a nail flush without marring wood surfaces, is the best one for your purposes. Long-handled hammers provide more leverage than short ones and are more suitable for framing work, but an average-sized handle will give you plenty of leverage for the standard container—even a container 24 inches square. Also, it is a good idea to have a *short*-handled hammer for the finishing work. The head of this hammer should weigh about 16 ounces.

The screwdriver is an important tool because containers last longer if they are screwed together. Buy three basic screwdrivers: a screwdriver with a square shank; a long screwdriver, which gives you more leverage than a short one; and a small screwdriver for working in tight places like corners. An ill-fitting screwdriver is always a headache. If the tip is too large for the screws' heads, for example, the screwdriver will mar the surface of the wood.

You can also now buy magnetized screwdrivers, which greatly reduce the possibility of the screwdriver tip slipping from the screw head.

If you are building a wood container, you will certainly need a handsaw; a power saw is really not necessary. The shape, number of teeth, and blade size determine the type of cutting a saw will do. The crosscut saw is probably the most popular; this saw is made to cut across the wood grain, and it can cut both plywood and hardwoods. A 20-inch saw and a smaller saw for detail work are basically all you will need for making containers. If you are cutting patterns, use what is called a coping saw.

For outside detailing or scoring, you will need chisels. Chisels make small grooves and cuts in wood. Most of them are driven with a hammer. A set of four chisels in blade widths of ¼, ½, ¾, and 1 inch is fine. When you are doing chisel work, use light taps with the hammer and remove the wood in small stages, a step at a time.

The Miter Box   Moldings cover many mistakes, and most boxes look best when capped with a molding. The best tool for making moldings is a miter box. With this inexpensive gadget you can cut the precise forty-five-degree angles needed for joining moldings together. The miter box comes with the forty-five-degree-angle saw slot; you apply the wood molding against the framing edge, and with a backsaw (square-type saw) make your cuts—an easy, effectual way of cutting precisely and accurately.

Nails   There are so many different types of nails that you should carefully look over the selection at your hardware store. The right nail for the right job is important. Ordinary nails come in bright and galvanized finishes and are designated as box, casing, common, or scaffold nails. For your purposes the common nail is satisfactory, although the box nail is somewhat better because it is less likely to split the wood. For finishing work use the finishing, or casing, nail.

Standard box and casing nails come in sizes from 2-penny to 16-penny. Once, long ago, the term "penny" meant the cost of a hundred nails—a

Quarter-Circle Container

Drawing 10

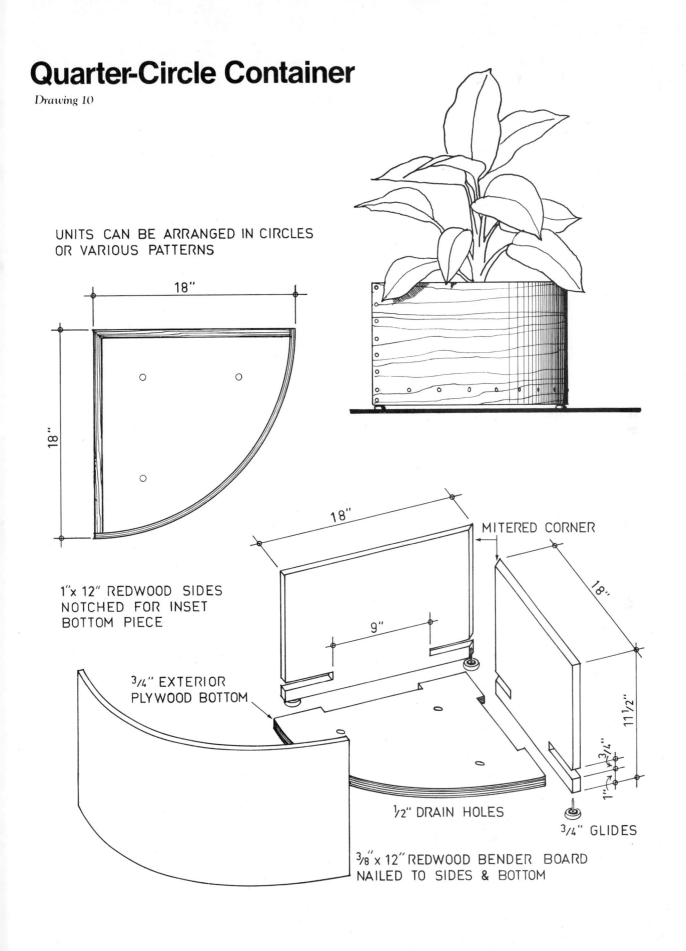

UNITS CAN BE ARRANGED IN CIRCLES
OR VARIOUS PATTERNS

18"

18"

18"

MITERED CORNER

18"

9"

11½"

¾"

1"

1"x 12" REDWOOD SIDES
NOTCHED FOR INSET
BOTTOM PIECE

¾" EXTERIOR
PLYWOOD BOTTOM

½" DRAIN HOLES

¾" GLIDES

⅜" x 12" REDWOOD BENDER BOARD
NAILED TO SIDES & BOTTOM

These long, stacked planters can be used as window boxes or on the patio. Note the lips that have been added, to give a more finished look. (Photo by Matthew Barr.)

hundred of the *smallest* nails cost two pennies. Today, the term indicates the length of the nail.

Glues and Epoxies   Wood glues and epoxies come in a wide variety; enough to confuse the average buyer. Glue applied at the corners of containers adds strength; and epoxy will hold joints together practically forever.

The animal or fish glues are most satisfactory when making indoor containers, where the temperature and humidity do not vary widely. A white glue known as polyvinyl glue is also used in making containers, but for a very strong waterproof joint you will need a resorcin resin. This is one of the most durable glues for outdoor-container usage. You must mix the powdered catalyst with liquid resin; then you have about ten minutes to form the joint after mixing the glue. Ask your hardware dealer for particulars.

Epoxies for wood are also generally easy to use. Drying time varies for these adhesives, and clamps may be necessary to hold the wood pieces together until the epoxy sets. Again, ask your hardware dealer for advice on the best one for the job.

No matter what kind of adhesive you use for bonding joints, be sure to ask for one that is waterproof.

Sanding Containers   To achieve the smooth finish that is most desirable, sand your container with the grain of the wood. Once sanded, the container can be used as it is, or (*especially* if it is to be used outdoors) then be coated with a clear finish or paint. Small belt sanders are available by rental and they do a fine job; or, if you prefer, you can make a sanding block by hand, by simply wrapping a piece of sandpaper around a block of wood.

There are, basically, three grades of sanding papers: garnet paper, which is reddish-black; aluminum oxide paper, which is black; and silicon carbide paper, which is rust-colored and the one most widely used. The three grades of paper come in various "grits," too. The "grit" is the density of the coating of the paper. Usually three densities of grit paper are necessary to achieve a smooth finish on wood, going gradually from the rougher (denser) grit to the finer. You can even do finer sanding if you like, but generally it is not necessary. The idea is to remove any flaws or defects in the wood in order to get a smooth, even finish.

The amount of sanding you do depends, furthermore, on the wood (type), the nature of the container (is it for outdoors or indoors?), and your personal preference. If the container is to have a clear finish, more sanding will be necessary than if it is to be painted—since paint will cover any mistakes or uneven surfaces.

Finishes and Paints   You can use any number of clear sealants and paints to finish containers. The paint or clear finish perfects them, with or even without their being detailed. And each, by the way, has its beauty. Some people say the unadorned box is more natural and more handsome than an embellished one. This is a matter of taste. I have seen beautiful detailed or painted boxes and I have also seen many fine examples of natural boxes with merely applied clear-sealant finishes.

There are numerous types of finishes on the market under different trade names, and it is therefore difficult to recommend a specific brand. A clear, tough finish is what you want; also, ask your paint dealer for a wood finish that *dries* quickly.

A finish protects the wood container and at the same time gives it a lustrous appearance. With any finish the trick is to brush it on evenly and smoothly. You can use one or two coats. It is a simple operation and goes a long way in protecting woods from wear.

You can also achieve a clear finish by using waxes on unfinished wood; the buildup of wax creates a protective finish that is handsome and lustrous. Various types of waxes are available at paint and hardware stores. Consult the dealer about what to use to achieve the type finish you want.

An infinite number of types of paint can be used on wood containers, and just what you select depends on your personal tastes. In any case, wood containers and wood housings should be sanded smooth before you apply the paint. Also, if the container is to be used outside, you will want outdoor-type paints. Indoors you may use enamels, etc.

4. Acrylic Containers

The relatively new world of plastics has opened new avenues to many fields, including containers for plants. Acrylic plastic is especially good for containers; this hard and durable material, while it can never replace wood, is easy to clean, lightweight, and fairly inexpensive.

Acrylic comes in several forms—cylinders, rods, sheets, etc.—and you can find suppliers in the yellow pages. For constructing containers, buy second-quality acrylic (it has some scratches) because the hairline marks are hardly noticeable.

You can make innumerable types of plant containers from acrylic: terrariums, hanging gardens, pedestals, trays, and on and on. Acrylic is truly a versatile product that requires little construction to turn it into what you want. For example, an acrylic *cylinder* becomes a plant stand in a matter of just a few minutes.

Do not scoff at acrylic as I did for many years. It has many uses as a plant container, so you are foolish if you do not take advantage of its possibilities.

Cylinders   Acrylic cylinders (or tubes) are hollow at each end, come in diameters of from 2 to 16 inches, and can be cut to order at any length. There are simple to elaborate ways to use an acrylic cylinder. Glue a disk to one end of the tube so the disk acts as a top; put a plant on the top. Presto—a plant stand. Or use the cylinder as is, as a sleeve, and rest the pot lip on the cylinder; put a drain saucer at the bottom and you have another plant stand. If you group three tubes of varying diameters together, you can easily create an island of greenery.

If you do not want to use a cylinder vertically, use a half-moon-shaped cylinder horizontally. Just glue two half-moon disks, one to each end of the cylinder, for a desk planter or a hanging planter.

You can also plant directly into an acrylic cylinder that has had a bottom applied to it.

Hanging Cylinders

Drawing 11

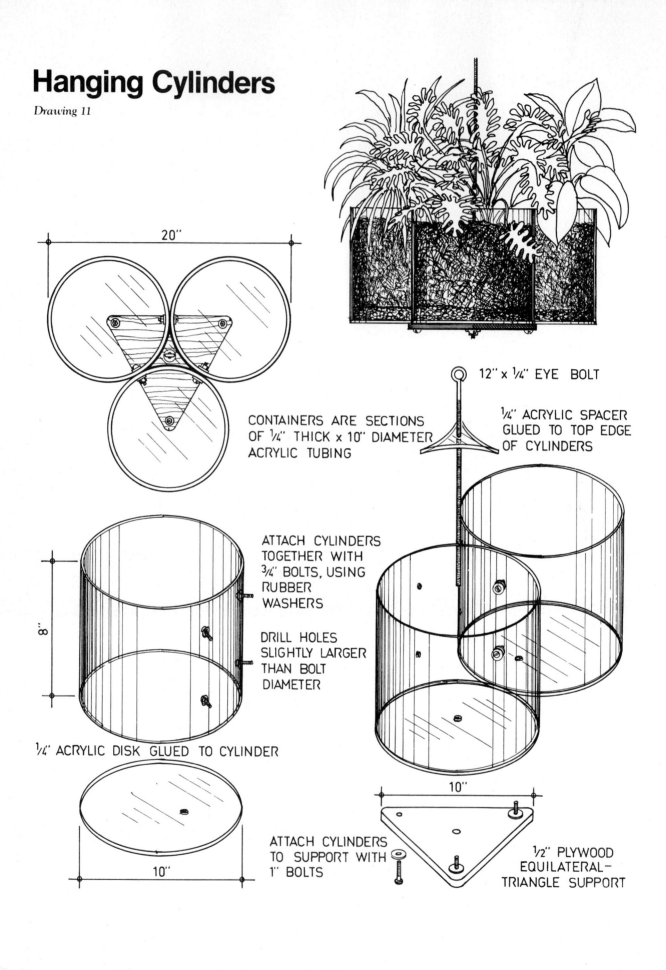

20"

CONTAINERS ARE SECTIONS
OF ¼" THICK x 10" DIAMETER
ACRYLIC TUBING

12" x ¼" EYE BOLT

¼" ACRYLIC SPACER
GLUED TO TOP EDGE
OF CYLINDERS

ATTACH CYLINDERS
TOGETHER WITH
¾" BOLTS, USING
RUBBER
WASHERS

DRILL HOLES
SLIGHTLY LARGER
THAN BOLT
DIAMETER

8"

¼" ACRYLIC DISK GLUED TO CYLINDER

10"

10"

ATTACH CYLINDERS
TO SUPPORT WITH
1" BOLTS

½" PLYWOOD
EQUILATERAL-
TRIANGLE SUPPORT

Acrylic, sold at plastic sheet supply houses, comes in several shapes and sizes. Here we see cylinders, sheets, rods, and disks. (Photo by Clark Photo.)

Sheets You can make a rectangular acrylic container from five pieces of acrylic sheet. All you have to do is join the pieces together with liquid-plastic cement, and in no time you have a plant container—a terrarium. Use an additional piece of acrylic (somewhat larger than the diameter of the terrarium) as a top.

A 12-inch, five-piece, cube pedestal or plant container takes one sheet of 12 x 12-inch material, two sheets of 12 x 11¾, and two 12½ x 11¾ sheets. Assemble the acrylic cube with plastic cement. Glue one side at a time. Or first tape the container or stand lightly together, and then with a small paintbrush or eyedropper insert the clear sealant along the edges. The cement makes a tight bond. Allow at least twelve hours for complete drying, before planting in the container or displaying on the stand.

Acrylic Lamp Cubes Occasionally I have been able to buy seconds (scratched) of acrylic lamp cubes at electrical supply stores or lamp shops. The cubes, open at both ends, come in three sizes: 8, 12, and 16 inches square. They make ideal hanging containers if one end is sealed with a plastic or clay dish or circle. I use a waterproof epoxy to cement a small saucer to the opening. Leave the other opening free so you can plant into the cube.

Whether we call these plant stands or plant containers, acrylic cylinders offer a unique way to display plants. (Photo by Clark Photo.)

Acrylic Stand

Drawing 12

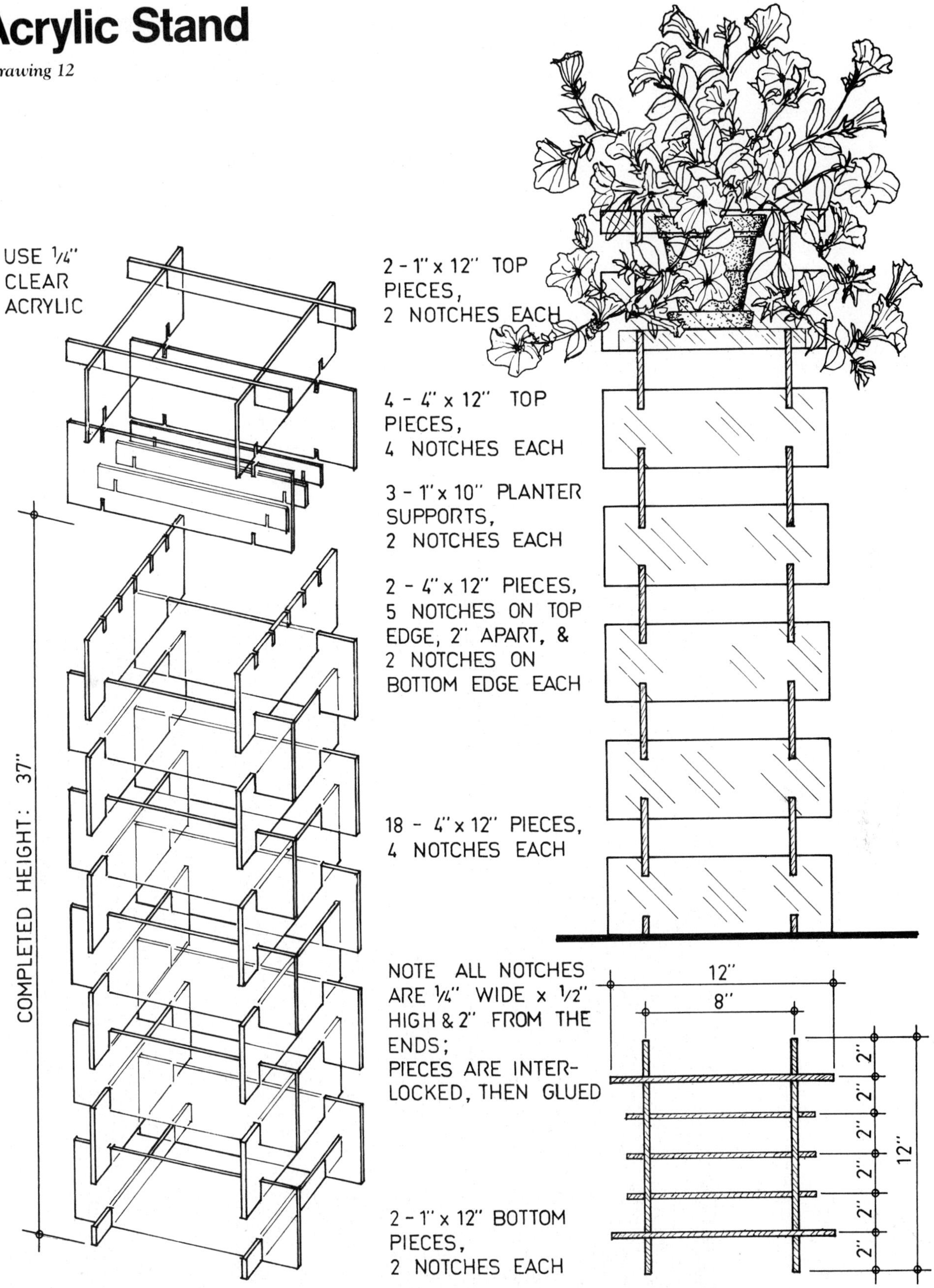

USE 1/4"
CLEAR
ACRYLIC

COMPLETED HEIGHT: 37"

2 - 1" x 12" TOP
PIECES,
2 NOTCHES EACH

4 - 4" x 12" TOP
PIECES,
4 NOTCHES EACH

3 - 1" x 10" PLANTER
SUPPORTS,
2 NOTCHES EACH

2 - 4" x 12" PIECES,
5 NOTCHES ON TOP
EDGE, 2" APART, &
2 NOTCHES ON
BOTTOM EDGE EACH

18 - 4" x 12" PIECES,
4 NOTCHES EACH

NOTE ALL NOTCHES
ARE 1/4" WIDE x 1/2"
HIGH & 2" FROM THE
ENDS;
PIECES ARE INTER-
LOCKED, THEN GLUED

2 - 1" x 12" BOTTOM
PIECES,
2 NOTCHES EACH

12"

8"

2"
2"
2"
2"
2"
2"
2"
12"
2"

Square acrylic containers are easy to make; glue five pieces of sheet together, and presto—a container for your plants (and it costs little). (Photo by Clark Photo.)

A distinctive stand or platform is this homemade acrylic unit that holds two potted plants. Its bottom provides space for pebbles; covered from time to time with water, they help create humidity for the plants. (Photo by Clark Photo.)

There is a certain elegance about the shape and color of acrylic lamp cubes and they blend well with contemporary interiors. Plants look good in the cubes, living in an almost terrarium-type atmosphere. You can set the cubes on desks or tables, but they really look their best as hanging planters (see Chapter 6 for how to make a hanging container).

Rods   Acrylic rods are solid pieces of acrylic in several diameters. The rod imparts an elegant effect. You can glue rods vertically to a flat wood surface, or use rods (of about 6 inches in diameter) as platforms for containers. Rods can also be used as supporting devices for hanging containers. Turning the rod horizontally, anchor it to the wall; then use monofilament wire to hang your plant containers from the rod.

Working with Acrylic   Buy acrylic cut to size rather than in large sheets, for these are hard to handle. You do pay a bit more for the cutting, but it is worth it—especially if you do not have many tools and only limited space in which to work.

Cover your work surface while working with acrylic, and leave the acrylic's protective adhesive paper on as long as possible.

Wood-and-Acrylic Container

Drawing 13

TOP & BOTTOM RAILS ARE 2 x 2's, EDGES HAVE
¼" x ¼" RABBETS FOR ACRYLIC SIDES,
CORNERS ARE MITERED

VERTICAL SUPPORTS ARE 2 x 2's; THE ACRYLIC
IS ATTACHED TO THE INSIDE WITH SCREWS &
RUBBER WASHERS

USE REDWOOD OR CEDAR

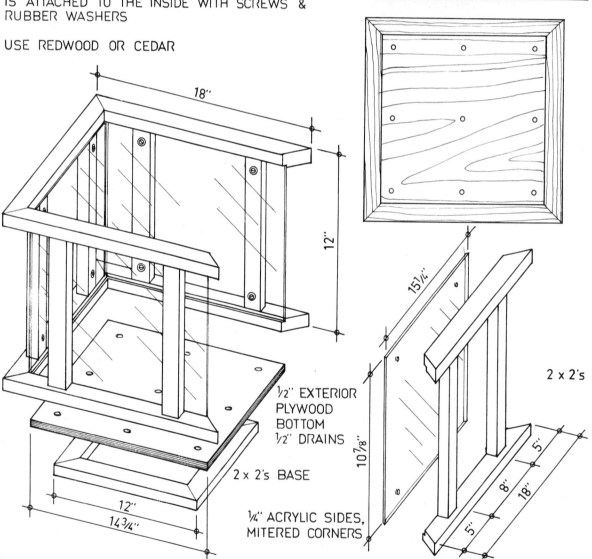

18"

12"

15¼"

10⅞"

½" EXTERIOR
PLYWOOD
BOTTOM
½" DRAINS

2 x 2's BASE

12"

14¾"

¼" ACRYLIC SIDES,
MITERED CORNERS

2 x 2's

5"

5"

8"

18"

5"

Cutting   If you chose to cut your own acrylic pieces, cut thin sheets with a scriber (sold at plastic suppliers). Use a steel rule to guide the cut, and work on an absolutely level surface. Repeat the scribe cut several times, and then lay the sheet, scribe-cut side up, on a wood dowel or wood pencil. (Be sure the wood prop is as long as the sheet.) Hold the sheet steady against the prop with one hand, and apply pressure with the other hand. Work both your hands along the cut as the break progresses. Thick sheets of plastic (over 3/16 inch) must be cut with a hand or electric saw. Practice a bit first on scrap pieces. Saw slowly and accurately—especially with an electric saw—to minimize vibration.

Sealing   The adhering process is easy but must be done slowly and carefully. Do not use just any adhesive; use a plastic sealant liquid that actually becomes part of the plastic, once it is applied: EDC or MDC. Mark the acrylic with a red grease pencil at the points where another piece is to join it. Apply the liquid with a small paintbrush or eyedropper—only in this marked-off area. The adhesive will first flow between the pieces to be joined, and after a few seconds harden and become part of the acrylic. Use light pressure for the first few seconds in order to bond the pieces; with time the bond becomes strong.

You can hold pieces in place while you are cementing them. However, it is better to tape them at the corners, so that there is less room for error and a stronger bond will be formed.

5. Terrariums

A terrarium is a closed glass (sometimes acrylic) case for growing plants in a miniature landscape or tiny greenhouse situation. Terrariums are beautiful scenes and provide almost ideal conditions because they produce (actually retain) their own moisture. The plant leaves release moisture that condenses on the inside of the glass and runs back down into the soil; this cycle repeats itself over and over again.

You can make terrariums in all kinds of shapes and sizes. Just remember to keep a balance between the air and soil space in the case and the number of plants; there must be the right amount of air and soil. A good size for a rectangular terrarium is 16 x 20 x 12 inches. Use six or nine small plants.

Glass Terrariums

Making glass terrariums is simple. First, have a glass shop cut the panes of glass to size. For a 16 x 20 x 12-inch terrarium you will need ¼-inch glass sheets cut into two 12 x 16 sides, two 12 x 20 sides, and one 16 x 20-inch bottom. The top piece should be 16 ½ x 20 ½ inches. Set up the four sides of the terrarium and seal them at the corners with waterproof epoxy; then use masking tape at the corners to help hold the glass in place until the cement dries. Another design is a compartmented terrarium made of wood and glass (see Drawing 15). The framework is made by wood dowels; panes of glass (or acrylic) form the sides and interior compartments.

For a different kind of terrarium you might want to make a stained-glass unit. Here's how to make one of these handsome containers: Draw your design on a piece of paper. The drawing should show the shape of each piece of glass to its actual size, and the pieces should be numbered for identification. Using carbon paper, trace the design onto thin cardboard about the stiffness of a manila folder (available at craft shops). Mark the cardboard with the same identifying numbers that appear on the design. Cut the cardboard into pieces so that you have a cardboard shape that matches the shape of every piece of glass in the design. Place the cardboard (one piece at a time) on the glass and outline it with a colored grease pencil; then cut out each piece of glass. Wrap a strip of copper foil (rolls of foil are available in

A wall-mounted stained-glass terrarium. The construction process and materials are the same as for any other terrarium. (Photo by Matthew Barr.)

craft shops) around the edge of each piece of glass. Assemble the foil-wrapped pieces of glass to form the design by laying the pieces on the paper on which the design was drawn. Apply solder flux to the foil on adjacent pieces of glass. Solder together the pieces one at a time.

To make a stained-glass terrarium, you will need: stained glass, paper to trace your design on, carbon paper, thin cardboard, ⅛-inch solid-core solder, a roll of ¼-inch copper foil, an inexpensive soldering iron (approximately $3), and soldering flux. All these supplies are available at hardware or craft stores. The photographs in this section should help you to make your own terrarium.

As mentioned, first you must cut the glass. You can easily do this with an ordinary glass cutter. Put a piece of used carpet on top of a flat surface—a table, for example. Now dip the cutter in oil, and make scorings on the glass. Use some, but not too much, pressure when scoring the cuts. Once the glass is scored, break it by applying pressure with your palms to each side of the score. If you are cutting small pieces of stained glass, put a wood dowel or pencil under the glass and then apply pressure with your palms. There is a knack to cutting glass, and it takes some experience to do it properly. Practice on scrap pieces; in time you will get the hang of it.

Making a stained-glass terrarium: Using a glass cutter, score the glass along the pattern line. Insert a dowel or a wood pencil under the scoring, and break the glass carefully by applying pressure on either side of the scoring. (Photo by Matthew Barr.)

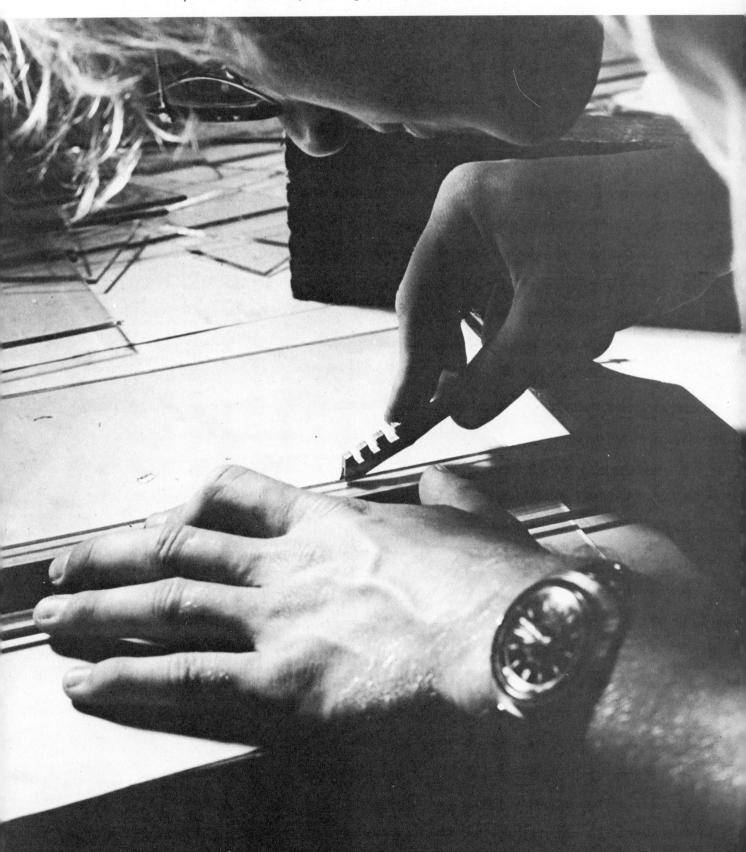

Wrap copper foil around the edges of the glass. (Photo by Matthew Barr.)

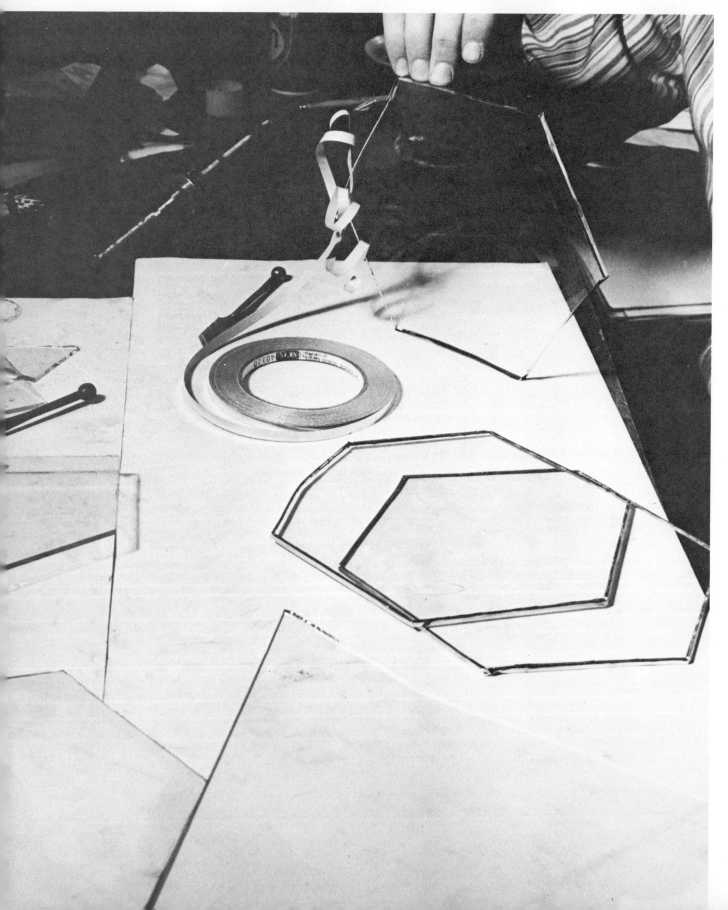

Apply solder flux to the foil on adjacent pieces of glass. (Photo by Matthew Barr.)

Solder the pieces together one at a time. (Photo by Matthew Barr.)

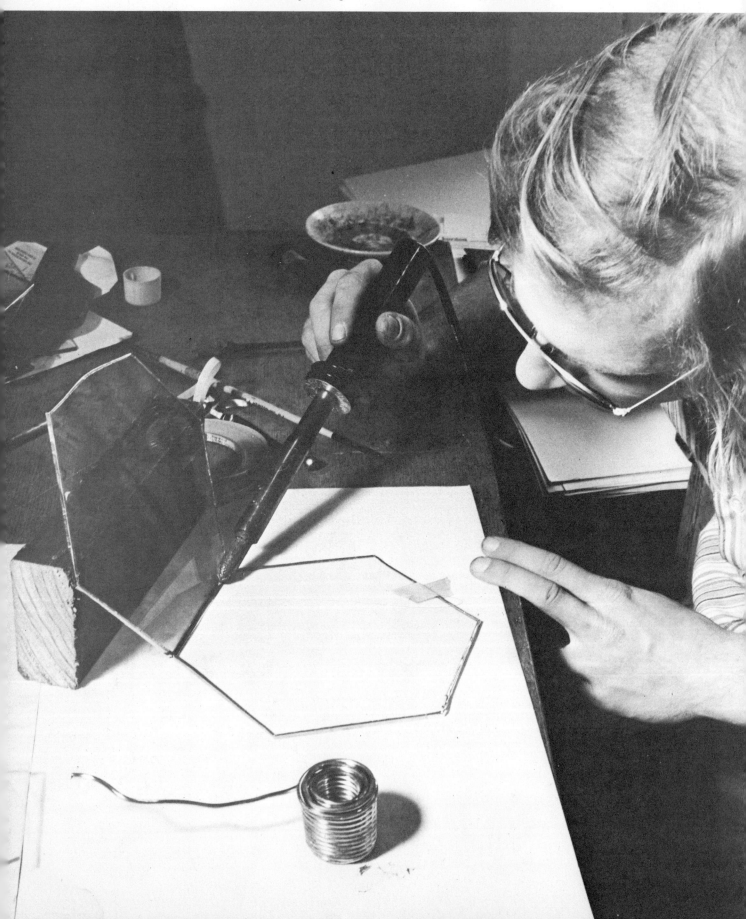

Wood-and-Glass Terrarium

Drawing 14

USE 2"x 6" REDWOOD OR CEDAR

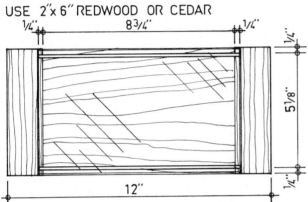

¼"   8¾"   ¼"

¼"

5⅛"

¼"

12"

APPLY WATERPROOFING SEALER TO WOOD
SURFACES; THE INTERIOR SHOULD HAVE
SEVERAL COATS

THE GLASS SIDES SHOULD BE AFFIXED
WITH CLEAR SILICONE RUBBER

⅛" PLATE-GLASS TOP & SIDES;
EXPOSED EDGES SHOULD BE POLISHED

9¼"   5½"

TOP FITS LOOSELY
IN ¼" x ¼" RABBET
CUTS

9¼"

10⅜"

45°

GLASS FITS IN ⅛" WIDE
x ¼" DEEP DADO, ¼"
FROM THE EDGE

USE WATERPROOF GLUE AT MITERED JOINTS

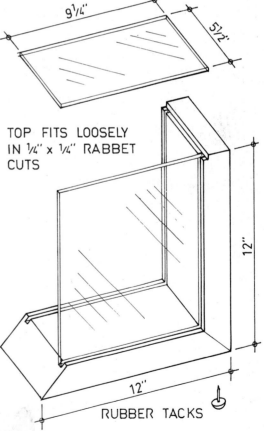

12"

12"

RUBBER TACKS

Dowel-and-Glass Terrarium

Drawing 15

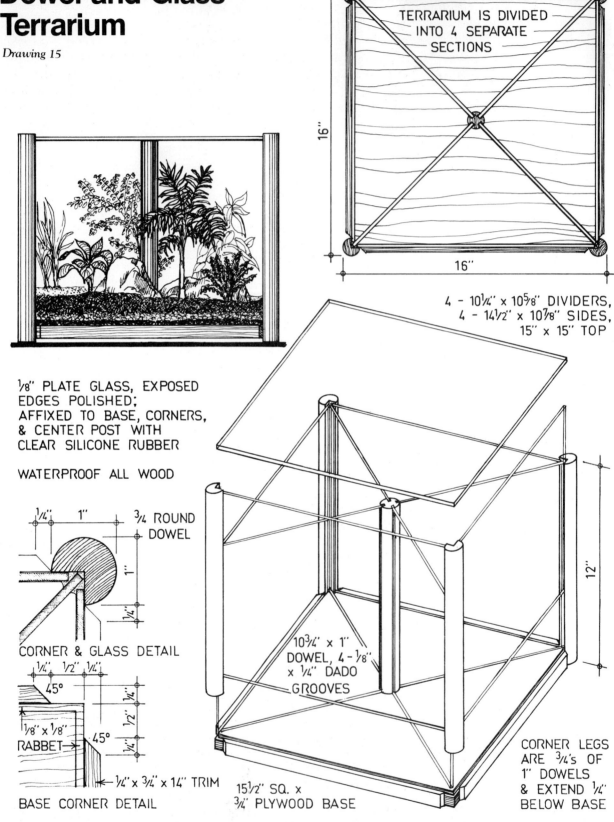

TERRARIUM IS DIVIDED INTO 4 SEPARATE SECTIONS

16"

16"

4 - 10¼" x 10⅝" DIVIDERS,
4 - 14½" x 10⅞" SIDES,
15" x 15" TOP

⅛" PLATE GLASS, EXPOSED
EDGES POLISHED;
AFFIXED TO BASE, CORNERS,
& CENTER POST WITH
CLEAR SILICONE RUBBER

WATERPROOF ALL WOOD

¼" 1" ¾ ROUND DOWEL

1"

¼"

CORNER & GLASS DETAIL

¼" ½" ¼"
45°
¼"
½"
⅛" x ⅛"
RABBET
45°
¼"
¼" x ¾" x 14" TRIM

BASE CORNER DETAIL

15½" SQ. x
¾" PLYWOOD BASE

10¾" x 1"
DOWEL, 4 - ⅛"
x ¼" DADO
GROOVES

12"

CORNER LEGS
ARE ¾'s OF
1" DOWELS
& EXTEND ¼"
BELOW BASE

Acrylic Terrariums   It is best to buy acrylic pieces precut to size in order to eliminate the need for tools and exact cutting. Like the glass terrarium, the acrylic case is basically four sides cemented together, a bottom panel cemented to the four sides, and a removable top. Or you can use five pieces of acrylic; in this case, cement the pieces together, and then invert the terrarium over a shallow wood box that has a galvanized metal tray insert. This slightly elevates the terrarium. Placed on a wooden pedestal for more elevation, the total is a handsome display.

Another simple acrylic terrarium is a 10-inch-diameter cylinder cemented to a plywood base; the top should, as usual, be removable. This attractive-looking terrarium takes only about ten minutes to make and provides you with a charming transparent miniature garden rather than the usual rectangular-shaped one.

Terrariums from Salvaged Materials   You can also make terrariums from such salvaged items as old milk jars, jugs, peanut butter jars, and pickle jars. Any jar or jug you use should be clear so you can see through it and should have an opening that you can fit plants through. Wine bottles are unsatisfactory because their small opening limits drastically what plants you can get into the bottle. Chemical flasks (if they are wide-mouthed) and beakers are other excellent terrarium possibilities; you might be able to salvage one, but pharmaceutical supply houses sell them (consult the yellow pages). See also Chapter 7.

Using a wood box as base and container for these plants, an acrylic "sleeve" has been placed over it to make a handsome terrarium. (Photo by Matthew Barr.)

6. Containers for Hanging Plants

The hobby of growing hanging plants has spawned dozens of unique hanging containers. Years ago the only commercial hanging container was a wire one, but now you can buy different kinds or make your own hanging containers in a multitude of designs. Making your containers is easy; just be sure you include some facility for catching drain water and be certain to use the proper supporting devices. So let us now actually discuss the many kinds of hanging planters and how to make them.

Wood Containers

Wood is *the* accepted material for handmade hanging plant containers. The most popular design is the crosshatched wooden basket, which can be made in several ways. For example, such a container can be a box within a box. Use ¾-inch dowels for the exterior box, and run 1 x 2-inch lathing horizontally on the outside, spaced ¼ inch apart. The laths should be 2 inches longer than the width of the box, so that there is a 1-inch overlap at each end.

If you are handy with tools, you can build a slotted redwood basket. Notch wood strips at each corner and join them together like a log cabin; that is, each railing notches into the other. Use wood epoxy to seal the joints at the corners.

The hanging wood container can also be a simple square or rectangular frame with an opening for a terra-cotta pot and saucer. Make this container from four redwood posts, a plywood base, and an insert panel to hold the pot lip or set the pot on the base. Drill holes into the top of the posts to hold eyelets for chain or wire.

Finally, you can make wood hanging containers in hexagon, triangle, or diamond shapes—of various sizes. There is amazing versatility in wood, so you can really use your imagination.

Remember that there will be excess water draining from any hanging pot. If the container is outside, this is not a problem; but for indoor use you should insert a clay saucer within the hanging container. The wood box will act as a cover-up for it.

Cutout Hanging Box

Drawing 16

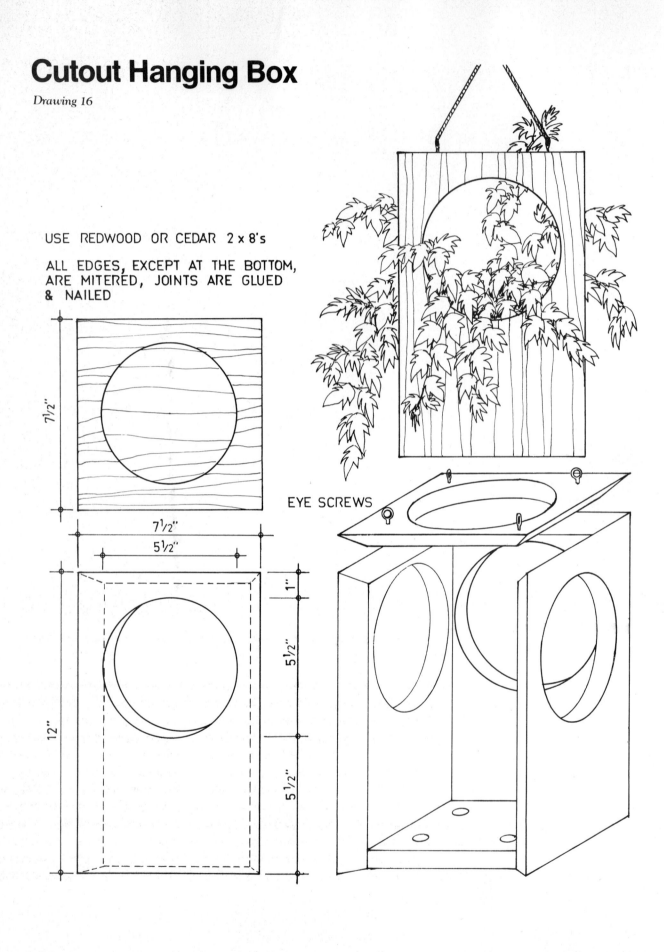

USE REDWOOD OR CEDAR 2 x 8's

ALL EDGES, EXCEPT AT THE BOTTOM, ARE MITERED, JOINTS ARE GLUED & NAILED

7½"

7½"

5½"

1"

5½"

5½"

12"

EYE SCREWS

Acrylic Containers   The easiest-to-make acrylic hanging container is the rectangular box (four sides, a bottom, and a top), with a round cutout for the pot. The pot rim rests in the hole, and water drains into the bottom, which should be filled with fine gravel chips so water can evaporate. String wires through predrilled holes at the edges in order to hang the container.

An acrylic cylinder cut in half, with two half-moon ends cemented in place (as mentioned previously), is yet another idea for a unique acrylic container. Drill holes at the ends, at the top of the half-moons, to run wire supports for ceiling hooks.

Hanging containers can be of many designs. The one at the right of the photograph is made of wood boards, and potted plants have been set inside it. (Photo by Matthew Barr.)

Wire baskets make ideal hanging containers, either for potting directly (when lined with sphagnum) or, as in this photograph, with potted plants set inside them. (Photo by Matthew Barr.)

Another unique hanging device is what I call the disk tray. Order precut circles (or disks) from suppliers (you can use 6- or 8-inch-diameter circles). Drill four ¼-inch holes at the edge of each circle, equidistant from each other, and string monofilament wire through the holes to hold the disks (like a hammock). With these units each circle holds one potted plant, and the weight of the pot steadies the tray. A similar design can be made by using a shallow round tray with predrilled holes in a larger tray that holds the shallow one.

Planting Hanging Containers
If you are using a wood or acrylic hanging container with drainage holes, follow the potting procedures explained in Chapter 12. For containers without drainage holes, insert a thin layer of crushed gravel in the bottom; use uneven-edged gravel so the water will have many surfaces to evaporate on. Also, put in a handful of charcoal chips to keep the soil sweet. Then add soil. Make pockets for the plants, and firm the soil around their collars.

Wire Baskets
You can make your own wire baskets, or buy commercial ones. To make your own, just create a design and then cut (with wire snips) and weave the wires together; or use a soldering iron to seal the crosspieces. This takes some time, but it can be done.

You can also just *bend* (heavier) wires together to form a basket. This at first makes a crude-looking housing, but with wire pliers it is easy to do and looks fine after a while—eventually the plants and the "lining" of the basket (sphagnum moss) hide the wires.

Follow these five steps for planting both commercial and homemade wire baskets:

1. Soak some sphagnum moss (a standard package) for a few hours and then line it into the bottom and sides of the basket. Slightly push the sphagnum through the wires so that it holds in place. (Sphagnum moss is sold loose or in sheets at nurseries.)

2. When the basket is fully lined, overlap the sphagnum at the top in order to form a shoulder.

3. Let the sphagnum dry. Then trim away the excess odd pieces of moss.

4. Fill the container with the packaged potting soil, and make pockets for the plants.

5. Set the plants in place; firm the soil around their collars and water the plants thoroughly.

A unique pottery hanging container. (Photo by Matthew Barr.)

Octahedral Hanging Basket

Drawing 17

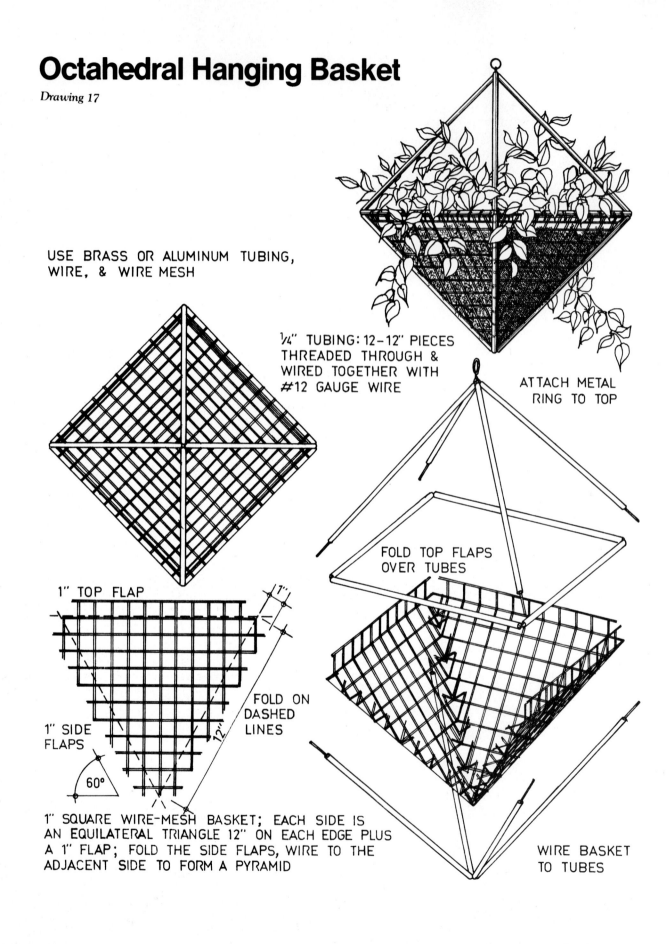

USE BRASS OR ALUMINUM TUBING, WIRE, & WIRE MESH

¼" TUBING: 12–12" PIECES THREADED THROUGH & WIRED TOGETHER WITH #12 GAUGE WIRE

ATTACH METAL RING TO TOP

FOLD TOP FLAPS OVER TUBES

1" TOP FLAP

1" SIDE FLAPS

60°

FOLD ON DASHED LINES

7"

12"

WIRE BASKET TO TUBES

1" SQUARE WIRE-MESH BASKET; EACH SIDE IS AN EQUILATERAL TRIANGLE 12" ON EACH EDGE PLUS A 1" FLAP; FOLD THE SIDE FLAPS, WIRE TO THE ADJACENT SIDE TO FORM A PYRAMID

A macramé sling holds this hand-painted pottery hanging container. (Photo by Matthew Barr.)

**Supports and
Hanging Devices**

Standard S-hooks, available in many sizes at hardware stores, are perfect for suspending plants from ceilings. First put eyelets or toggle bolts (also available at hardware stores) into the ceiling. (Screw eyelets into *wood* ceilings; drill holes for toggle bolts in *plaster* ceilings.) From the eyelet or toggle bolt suspend the S-hook. Now attach or tie monofilament wire securely from the hook. You may also want to consider those toggle bolts made specifically for hanging plants. These come in white, black, or gold. You first put in the bolt, and then screw on the decorative hook. Some of the devices rotate, so you can turn the plants with the sun. Other types have a pulley to enable you to lower your hanging plants for watering.

There are several ways to connect a container to a hook. Three chains, wires, or strings can be brought together in one point and hooked or tied onto the S-hook. You can also use a dog-leash lock spring in the ceiling to hold plants from an S-hook, or a fishing-tackle swivel between two S-hooks.

For a plant weighing less than twenty-five pounds, and set in a flat-based container, you can use an inexpensive acrylic platform. The container sits on the platform, which is suspended by four monofilament wires that are joined to form a loop. Hook the loop onto an S-hook.

If you want to hang more than one plant to the same support, secure a solid acrylic rod into two adjoining walls, about 4 inches down from the ceiling. Use S-hooks on the rod, or loop wire around the rod to hold planters. To hang plants from your walls, rather than your ceilings, use a wrought-iron arm (any hardware store or plant shop carries them). Screw the arm to the wall and hang the pot from the end of the arm. Outdoors, try the clip-on pot holders that screw to fences or the sides of houses; just clip the container to the holder.

**Macramé as a
Supporting Device**

Macramé has enjoyed tremendous popularity recently and has appeared as hanging supports for plant containers. (See Drawing 31 for macramé-making.) I have seen an array of macramé hangers in an incredible number of designs and done in various types of yarn, rope, jute, rattan, and so on. You can make your own macramé plant hangers—many people do—or buy them ready-made at stores. The advantage of course in making your own is that you can create your patterns, and it is also easier thereby to create a permanent support for a *specific* container.

No matter whether you buy the macramé hanger or make your own, be sure it is durable and expandable enough to hold a plant container. An 8-inch pot filled with soil weighs about thirty pounds. You would not want the weight to slip and fall on someone's head, or lose the plant in an accident. So, again, I say: Be sure that the material you use is durable. Also, choose a design that is closely enough meshed so that it can hold the container securely.

There are many fine books on macramé if you decide to make your own hanging devices for your handcrafted containers.

Hexagonal Hanging Basket

Drawing 18

USE ¾" WOODEN DOWELS,
PAINTED OR WATERPROOFED

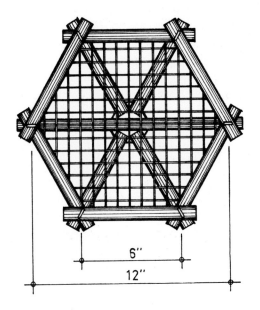

6"

12"

THE BASKET IS COMPOSED OF ¾"
x 8" OVERLAPPED DOWELS HELD
TOGETHER WITH EYE BOLTS AT
THE INTERSECTIONS

THE BOTTOM PIECES ARE WIRED
TOGETHER AT THE CENTER &
THE ENDS ARE ATTACHED WITH
THE EYE BOLTS;
¾" MESH IS LAID OVER

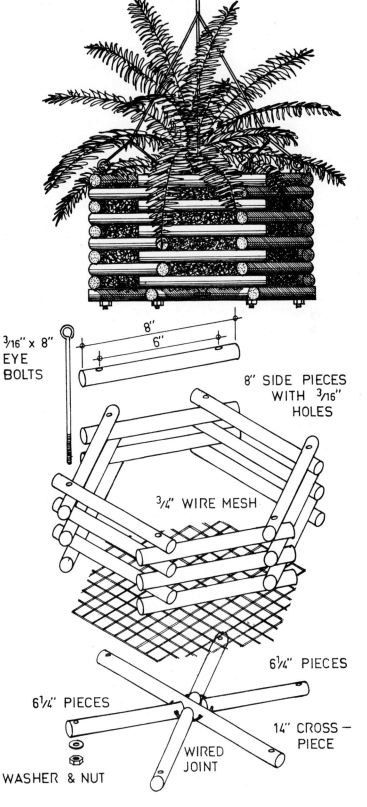

³/₁₆" x 8"
EYE
BOLTS

8"

6"

8" SIDE PIECES
WITH ³/₁₆"
HOLES

¾" WIRE MESH

6¼" PIECES

6¼" PIECES

14" CROSS-
PIECE

WIRED
JOINT

WASHER & NUT

7. A Gallery of Containers

In the preceding chapters we have talked about more or less standard-type containers you can make, such as wood boxes and planters, glass and acrylic containers and terrariums, and hanging containers. This chapter presents many types of housings for plants that can be made from varied and assorted items such as seashells, bird cages, and other things that you just might not associate with containers.

Many of the make-it-yourself containers are highly decorative—bird cages, for example—and some are good because they just don't cost anything: coffee cans, for example. In this gallery of plant containers there is something for everyone—and a housing for almost any type of plant.

Coffee Cans
Coffee cans can be excellent free containers for your greenery. A grouping of plants set in decorated coffee cans is a sophisticated picture. By simply painting the cans or covering them with Con-Tact-type paper you create decorative housings for your plants.

Be sure to punch drainage holes in the can bottoms. Coffee comes in various size cans; each size can accommodate only an appropriate size plant. The two-pound can is ideal for most medium-sized plants.

A more elaborate coffee-can plant holder can be made from a square redwood box. The top and bottom of the box should be ½ inch thick. Cut an opening into the top, making the opening large enough to hold a coffee can. Place redwood posts under each corner of the box for elevation. Now insert the can into the opening.

Seashells and Driftwood
These natural materials can be handsome plant containers if they are suitable. For example, a *tiny* seashell is worthless because you cannot plant anything in it; and a piece of driftwood is suitable only if it has an interesting shape and design and is big or deep enough.

A shell should be large enough to accommodate the plant. But few shells are large enough, so if you want to use the beauty of a shell in combination with plants, use *miniature* plants. However, this container will be temporary

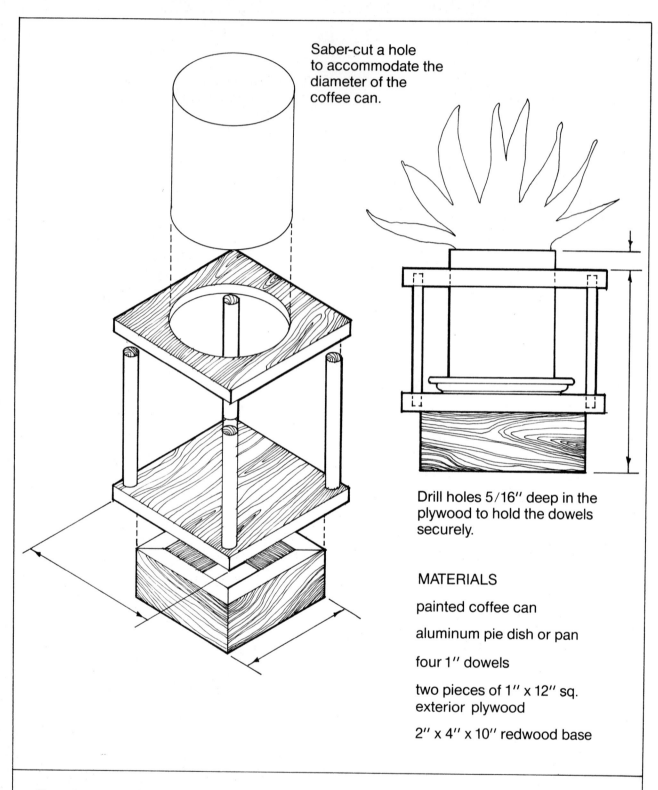

Saber-cut a hole
to accommodate the
diameter of the
coffee can.

Drill holes 5/16″ deep in the
plywood to hold the dowels
securely.

MATERIALS

painted coffee can

aluminum pie dish or pan

four 1″ dowels

two pieces of 1″ x 12″ sq.
exterior plywood

2″ x 4″ x 10″ redwood base

Coffee-Can Plant Housing

Drawing 19

1. Find a suitable large shell.

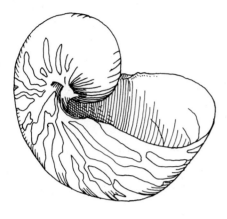

2. Put in a layer of soil; pack it in the corners with a blunt-nosed wood stick.

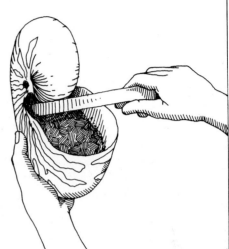

3. Insert a small plant; fill in and around it with soil.

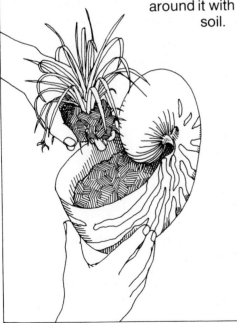

4. Water thoroughly.

Planting a Seashell
Drawing 20

because the amount of soil that can be used in a shell will not support plant life very long. The exceptions are abalone shells; these shallow but rather large shells can be home for lilliputian plants for years.

Look for gnarled, interesting driftwood, preferably a piece that already has a natural pocket for plants. (Most driftwood can be found on the beaches and shoreline after winter storms.) If you want to further bleach the driftwood—and therein is half its beauty—soak it several times in water with household bleach. Enlarge the pocket with a chisel so there is enough space for at least two cups of soil. For best results, plant the soil-filled pocket with small-leaved trailing plants such as ivy or philodendron. Driftwood pieces can be displayed as a piece of sculpture on a table, or hung on walls for dramatic effect.

Note: It is better to mist plants growing in driftwood rather than to pour water over them, because in time the soil will stagnate if watered directly.

A small piece of driftwood holds a tiny fern and a bromeliad. When locating pieces of driftwood, be sure they have natural pockets in them. (Photo by Matthew Barr.)

1. Select a balanced position for the driftwood and carve out or deepen a hole.

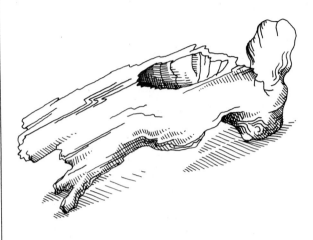

2. Fill the hole halfway with soil.

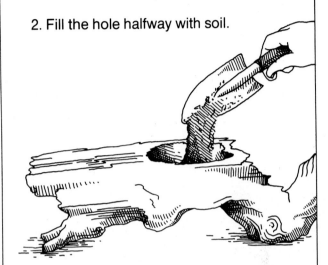

3. Insert a small plant and add more soil.

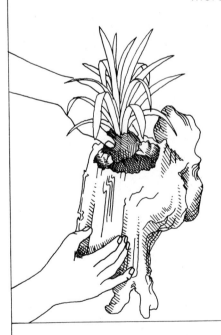

4. Water.

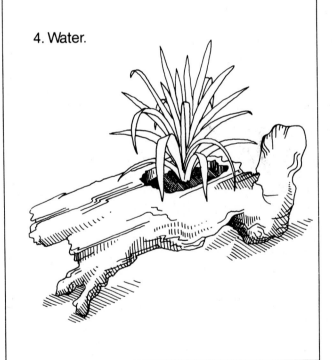

Planting Driftwood

Drawing 21

1. After cutting off the top fourth of the shell, drain and clean out its meat, leaving a clean shell.

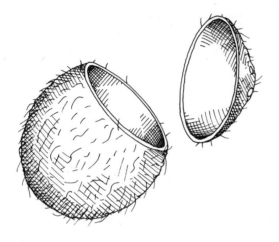

2. File the ends of the shell flat, and cement them together.

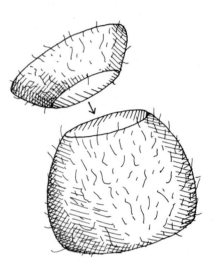

3. Fill the container half full of soil.

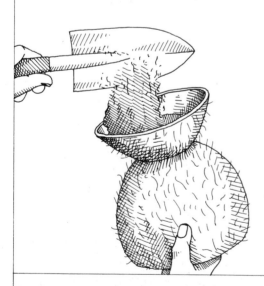

4. Insert a small plant; add more soil, and water.

Planting a Coconut
Drawing 22

Coconut Shells and Gourds

Years ago I used coconut shells for orchids because this was then considered a different way of growing these air plants—a way of stimulating growth. The method was different, but growth was not stimulated that much. The coconut shell is a natural container, and can be handsome with plants. The trouble is that the coconut shell is hard to cut. But this container *is* inexpensive and unique, so here is how to make it:

With a nail or ice pick, pierce the three eyes in the coconut end and drain the milk. (Do not throw away this delicious milk; drink it!) Cut the top fourth of the other end of the coconut—the end opposite the eyes—with a saw. Now, with a kitchen knife, lift out the meat inside the shell. This is not easy; nevertheless it can be done. But the object is to keep the shell intact. Once the shell has been scooped out, leaving it clean inside, plant it with soil. To keep the coconut upright, insert it in a shallow dish filled with sand—or prepare it as shown in Drawing 22.

Gourds have been used for centuries, usually as drinking containers. They are sold commercially as planters, but to make your own follow this method: Soak the gourd in water overnight, then remove the outside peel with a scouring brush. With a knife, carve out a planting hole, removing the seeds and inner membrane. Now sand off all uneven edges. Coat the inside of the gourd with melted paraffin, and spray the outside with a plastic sealer (available at hardware stores). Hang the gourd in a macramé sling or other support. This unique planter is worth the time and effort.

Philodendrons live in this gnarled piece of wood. (Photo by Matthew Barr.)

1. Scour off the outside peel of the gourd, cut a hole in it with a knife, and remove the seeds and membrane.

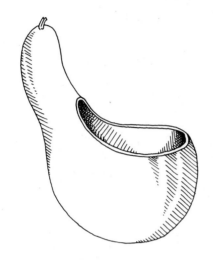

2. After coating the inside with melted paraffin, half fill the gourd with soil.

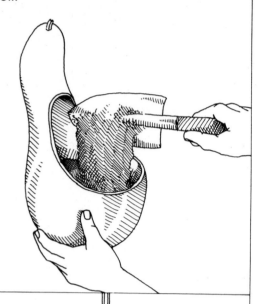

3. Insert a plant; add more soil and pack it in.

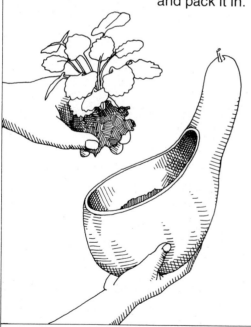

4. Water.

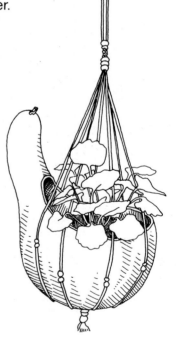

Planting a Gourd

Drawing 23

A healthy spider plant is growing in this hanging gourd. (Photo by Matthew Barr.)

Household Items   The household items that make the best plant containers are crocks, kitchen pots and pans, old pitchers, and lettuce baskets. The success of the kitchen-type container depends on the item itself. The blue-speckled-white metal pitcher is attractive; crocks in natural colors (available in several sizes at hardware and houseware stores) are stunning containers for plants; and most enameled kitchen pots and pans are decorative holders. (The wire lettuce basket is discussed later in this chapter.)

Household containers usually have no facility for drainage, however, so planting must be done carefully. Line the bottoms with charcoal in order to keep the soil sweet; and gravel, so excess water evaporates readily. Any of these kitchen items are fine for houseplants, or, if the container is shallow, for growing bulbs. And, lest I forget, my favorite kitchen container for plants is a bean pot; the lovely shape makes it an ideal plant holder.

An everyday household crock is used for a container in the corner of this sun room. (Photo by Joyce R. Wilson.)

Here a pickle jar doubles as a terrarium; the plants inside are tiny. This container is absolutely free.
(Photo by Joyce R. Wilson.)

Glass Jars, Jugs, Bowls, and Globes

The three-gallon pickle jar is good for terrariums because its opening is large enough for your hand. And with its top cut off, the jar can be a handsome container. Standard one-gallon fruit or vinegar jars, with small openings, are also fine containers. Cut these jars in half: the bottom can be planted with small plants, and the top half can be a hanging container when suspended upside down by a macramé sling and plugged at its mouth with a cork. Gallon jars are easy to find, but the three-gallon type are not so easy to find—ask your friendly grocer for some.

No matter what kind of jar or jug you use to make containers, you will have to buy a bottle-cutting kit. Follow the instructions enclosed with each kit—which generally are: Oil the cutter wheel and make the desired cut—a clean line on the glass—and pray. Four out of five times the glass cuts evenly. (Always allow for a broken jug.) Bottle cutting takes a fair amount of practice.

After you have cut the glass, place some aluminum foil or liquid leading around the top of the cut. This will protect you from cutting yourself when working with the container. Or use masking tape or any type of clear sealing tape to make a safe, neat band around the edges.

No jar or jug has drainage facilities and drilling holes in glass is tricky. So forget drilling holes; just be careful when planting the container. Before adding the soil, put in charcoal chips to keep it sweet; and use fine pulverized gravel to help evaporate any excess water.

Lighting centers carry an assortment of expensive glass bowls and globes. To save money, buy replacement globes (the type for old kerosene lamps) at an electrical supply house. I bought a clear round globe, 10 inches in diameter, for $5, and it made a perfect plant container. To keep the globe upright, put a layer of sand into a household dish and then insert the globe.

Tiles   Floor or mosaic tiles, in 6-inch squares, come in many designs and colors. Five tiles used together will make a pretty container; three tiled containers grouped together will give your indoor decor a strong impact.

You can cement together the five pieces of tile: four tiles for the sides and one for the bottom. However, I suggest you use a ½-inch-thick plywood base, instead, because it is much easier to drill drainage holes in wood than in tile. The plywood base will not detract from the appearance of the container.

Use a flat working surface such as a table or bench and protect the surface with newspaper or wax paper. Apply a ribbon of ceramic epoxy (purchased at tile outlets) along the edges of the tiles. Secure the pieces while the cement sets by using strips of masking tape at each corner.

Sewer and drain pipes like these come in many sizes and make suitable containers for plants. They may be used outdoors without a bottom, or indoors with a plywood bottom attached. (Photo by Matthew Barr.)

Tile Sewer Pipes and Flues

Sewer or drain pipes and flues, in tile or rigid plastic, are available at building supply yards. Sizes and shapes are as varied as are sewer connections, but believe me, there is a large world of plant containers to make from these inexpensive and attractive materials.

The regular double-hub 4-inch tile flue or pipe is terra-cotta in color and makes an original and handsome container. Outdoors, set the pipe on the ground, fill it with soil, and plant. Indoors you'll need a ¼-inch plywood base for the pipe. Other clay pipes, in diameters of 4, 5, or 6 inches, are *straight* cylinders (without the hub caps) and can also be used as is for pedestals, for outdoor planting, or, with a base, for attractive indoor plant containers.

The rigid plastic pipe available in various diameters comes in black or white and can be used in the same manner as clay pipes. Plastic has a sophisticated look that compliments many home interiors.

Concrete Blocks

Hollow-core concrete blocks are at lumberyards and it is worth a trip there to find them, because they are inexpensive and make fine outdoor plant housings. The blocks come in several sizes, usually 12 x 8 x 12 inches or 12 x 8 x 16 inches.

A flue liner can be a handsome plant container. Use it on your patio or in your garden; for indoor use, glue plywood to its bottom. (Photo by Matthew Barr.)

Standard concrete blocks can be used for outdoor containers; group some together, or stack them, for a container garden. (Photo by Matthew Barr.)

1. Choose a sewer pipe and flue as outdoor containers.

2. Fill each with soil to within six inches of its rim.

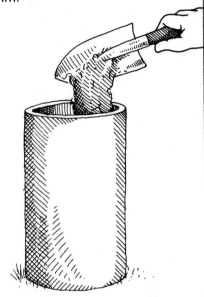

3. Insert a plant and add soil.

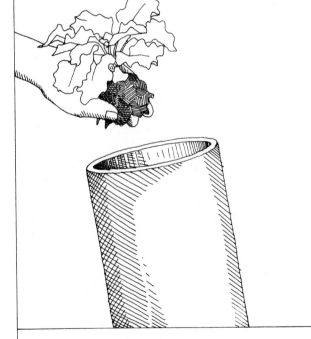

4. Water.

Planting a Sewer Pipe and Flue

Drawing 24

1. For your outdoor garden or patio, select a concrete block and fill the openings half full of soil.

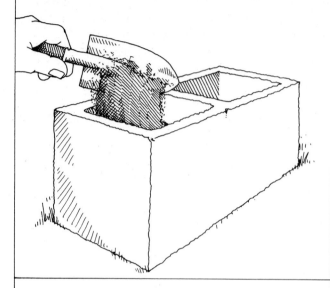

2. Insert small plants; fill in and around them with soil.

3. Water.

For indoors, place the block in a drip saucer.

Planting a Concrete Block

Drawing 25

This double-hub sewer pipe makes a striking container for plants. It is inexpensive and terra-cotta in color—and can also double as a plant stand. (Photo by Matthew Barr.)

They are set on the ground, filled with soil, and then can be planted. If you group several together, you can create a handsome container garden in a short time. You can also stack blocks one on top of the other for more planting depth. Concrete blocks lend themselves to many modular designs for patio or garden and their natural gray color usually harmonizes well with outdoor fixtures.

Kitchen-wire Baskets   There are numerous types of kitchen-wire baskets available at shops and people are using them effectively for plants rather than kitchen uses. Sometimes called lettuce baskets, these items require careful planting to become a satisfactory housing for hanging plants. Refer to Drawing 26 for planting an open wire basket.

You can also make your own wire basket from spool wire. The making of the wire basket is somewhat like basket weaving. Use a flexible wire (gauge 16) and, depending on the pattern you choose, the basket is hooked together by forming grasping or U-shaped ends and is further secured by braiding with wire. Study some of the commercial baskets before you attempt making your own. The design of the basket may be a simple grid (the most often used) or a more elaborate one, depending upon your skill. You will need wire snips and pliers, and if you are working with oval or curved patterns, a wood dowel to shape the wire on. Generally the wires are crimped at their end with pliers, to form the U-shaped ends.

Wire baskets may also be used to hold a potted plant. Commercial wire baskets may come with suitable hooks and hanging supports, so all you have to do is slot the clay pot into the basket for a cascading garden.

1. Lay a sheet of sphagnum around the inside of the basket; press it into place.

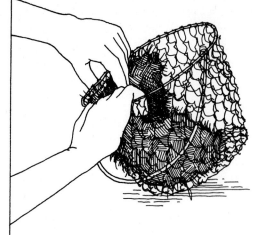

2. Fill the basket with soil, halfway.

3. Insert a plant and add more soil.

4. Water.

Planting a Lettuce Basket

Drawing 26

Bird Cages   Bird cages look fine in photographs but are not very practical as housings for plants. Most bird cages open from the bottom (for cleaning) and, like antique sewing machines sometimes used for plants, they have drawbacks. Once the plant is in the cage, it is difficult to water, the wires of the cage usually rust, and the cage becomes more a trap for the plant than a handsome housing.

If you do want to use them—and I admit they are decorative—the best idea is simply to set some shallow plant containers with cascading plants *inside* the cage. Do not plant directly into the bottom pan of the cage. However, if the bird-cage-as-a-container idea intrigues you and you want to do a finished piece, have a galvanized circular bin made for the bottom of the cage, at least 6 inches deep, and plant in this.

Bird cages are often used as plant containers, and are novel, but they require a planting pan inside or a galvanized-metal bottom. (Photo by Matthew Barr.)

Old wine barrels cut in half make ideal containers for large plants. (Photo by Matthew Barr.)

A simple clay mixing bowl, topped with a glass dome, makes a distinctive showplace for plants. (Photo by author.)

Washtubs, Nail Kegs, and Wine Barrels

When you think of a tub for a plant, a washtub immediately comes to mind and these do make fine outdoor containers for plants if they are brightly painted. Punch drain holes in the bottom of the tub. Other tubs suitable for plants are empty steel oil drums or rigid, plastic-coated, five-gallon ice-cream containers. However, ice-cream tubs are merely temporary because they are only made of heavy-duty cardboard. Eventually water will rot them.

Nail kegs and small wine barrels are sturdier ready-made tubs that need little modification to make them ideal for plants. You'll find that most barrels are already sawed in half at the midpoint; but if you get a barrel from a winery, it is easy to saw it yourself. Make a chalk mark around the belly of the barrel and saw along the mark. Shallow barrel halves, or ends, filled with

Here soy kegs are used as handsome plant containers. (Photo by Joyce R. Wilson.)

annuals and perennials look charmingly old-fashioned on patios and porches. Or you may saw the kegs or barrels in half *lengthwise* and fit them with pipes as legs; you will thereby have two long, shallow planters. Of course you may use the barrels uncut, if you find them so and desire the additional height.

Nail kegs and barrels come in several sizes. The 12- and 18-inch depths are the most suitable for many plants.

A few years ago most wine barrels and nail kegs were usually given away. But today these old-fashioned products are very much in demand, so they are no longer free. A sawed-in-half wine barrel can cost almost as much as a standard commercial plant container of comparable size. I recently bought a three-quarter barrel, about 30 inches in diameter, for planting a small tree; it cost $17.

Look for barrels or kegs that have galvanized hoops; those with black iron hoops must be painted or they will rust. (To locate barrels and kegs, look in the yellow pages.) Remember, too, to drill drainage holes before filling them with soil and plants.

Butter Drums and Soy Kegs

Used sixty-pound butter drums are especially handsome, but they are hard to find. The one possible container that has yet to be "discovered," and so is still worth the cheap price, is the soy keg. Soy kegs come in 10-, 12-, and 14-inch diameters. The wood is hard and durable, and the metal bands add an attractive finish to these containers.

8. Containers for Cuttings, Seeds, and Divisions

Most people who garden eventually try growing young plants, mainly to save money and to have the joy of raising their own "babies." And it does make good sense to grow your own plants from youngsters, because nature is free with her bounty. Even if you are not a professional gardener, you are bound to be successful with new plants from cuttings, seeds, and divisions.

My books *Grow Your Own Plants* (New York: Scribner's, 1975) and *Starting from Seed* (New York: Ballantine, 1977) outline the various ways of starting plants. Here I am going to discuss the types of containers you will need for the grow-your-own process. Cuttings and seeds have to be started in other than the "regular" containers; divisions can be planted in any type of container.

Cutting Containers

The most common way the average gardener starts a new plant is from a cutting: a 3- to 4-inch end of a mature plant. But a cutting should not be immediately planted in a standard pot of soil; first you want roots to form on a cutting. So start a cutting either in water, or in a growing medium called vermiculite, or in any standard packaged medium.

If you are starting a cutting in water, use a discarded mayonnaise jar, a small glass, or a small piece of pottery such as a teacup or coffee mug. Put some pebbles in the bottom of the container to anchor the end of the cutting securely. Or, if you want to spend the money, buy some cutting jars (sold at department stores and plant shops). These containers are quite delicate but attractive: round globes, abstract shapes, or animal shapes—all to be suspended from "invisible" monofilament wire. Cutting jars are worth the money if you want your cutting to be decorative, and these containers certainly look nicer than mayonnaise jars!

To grow cuttings in vermiculite or any other packaged medium, make shallow redwood boxes or use shallow but long (or wide) household items (soup tureens, roasting pans, casserole dishes, etc.) you can salvage (be sure these are at least 4 inches deep). If you make the boxes, they should be 4 inches deep x 16 inches wide x 20 inches long. This size box will hold dozens of cuttings. Be sure to put drainage holes in the bottom of the box.

Either homemade box or salvaged kitchen item should be large enough to hold at least a dozen cuttings.

Seed Containers   Growing seed is the most economical way of raising plants because you get a lot of seed for little money, and even if some seed do not germinate, most of the seed will, so you will have enough plants for your needs. The standard container for growing seed is the common "flat"—a wooden box with 4-inch-wide slats at the bottom. The slats are spaced ½ inch apart; the box is 3 inches deep. A flat is usually 16 inches wide and 20 inches long. Sometimes nurseries will sell you flats for a modest amount, but if you scrounge around at supermarkets that sell plants, you can often manage to get flats at no charge.

The flat is not your most attractive seed container, so you may want to make other, more appealing containers. A simple cedar or redwood box, 3 to 4 inches high and 12 inches square, works fine. But be sure you make holes in the bottom. Paint the outside of the box to give it some dimension and to enable it to blend with the decor of the room where you have placed it. By the way, the kitchen and the bathroom are good rooms to germinate seed in; they have extra humidity and warmth.

You can also start seed in any decorative shallow container you have on hand or make. Just be sure the container has a minimum depth of 4 inches and drainage holes at the bottom. An acrylic box is fun for starting seed because you can actually see the seed sprout and start growth. Children especially get a kick out of this way of growing seed.

"Flats," such as this one, are excellent for starting cuttings. You can get them at nurseries. (Here potted plants have been set within the flat.) (Photo by Matthew Barr.)

A commercially made glass bowl has been turned into a hanging container for starting cuttings.
(Photo by Matthew Barr.)

Containers for Divisions   A division is a part of a plant; you actually divide a plant to get a new whole one. This is done by slicing the plant in half (clear through) where you see a natural separation. A division is thus really a small plant in itself, so you can plant it in any type of container you wish: a homemade wood or acrylic container, a terra-cotta pot with a cover-up, etc. (Cover-ups are described in Chapter 11.)

9. Containers for Miniature and Small Plants

Small containers for dish gardens and bonsai are difficult to find but fun to look for. They are also easy to make—and the homemade item is distinctive and handsome. The popular hobby of bonsai is an art in itself, and dish gardening too is a special talent that can be easily learned by the ambitious plant lover. In each case, the container is as important as the total planting. You can even put miniature plants in teacups, gourds, coffee cans—whatever. This chapter covers container craft for such lilliputian gardens. Small plants such as peperomias and pileas make excellent candidates for tiny gardens.

Bonsai Dishes
You can buy the commercial bonsai dish in many sizes and shapes, and in brown or matte gray. These dishes are attractive, but more interesting containers can be made by even the amateur. Homemade bonsai dishes or boxes derive their beauty from original designs and shapes, and making these containers provides gardeners with a way of utilizing their talents.

The bonsai dish or box relies on simplicity and elegance of line to make the total effect harmonious.

A simple bonsai box is five pieces of redwood or cedar carefully mitered, sanded, painted, and joined, 5 to 6 inches deep and 8 to 10 inches square. The box may also be rectangular; a good rectangular size is 8 x 10 inches. Elevate the box by carefully attaching four shallow legs, one at each coner. All pieces of the box should be flush and even, with no roughness or lack of alignment. Apply a coat of clear resin to emphasize the handsome grain of the wood. Remember that the art of bonsai is perfection, and perfection applies to the container as well as the plants.

If you want to make a concrete bonsai dish, follow this procedure: Use two cardboard cartons and follow the directions in Drawing 27. The concrete mix for a bonsai dish should be fairly stiff; use three parts cement, one part sand, and two parts pebbles. Or use Sakrete commercial mix and just add water.

For bonsai uses, you might also want to search for unusual glazed dishes at

Concrete Bonsai Dish

Drawing 27

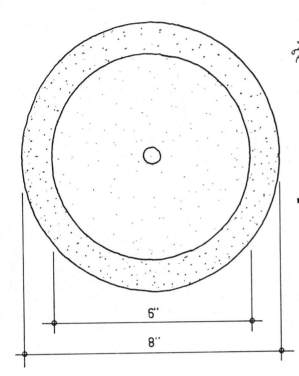

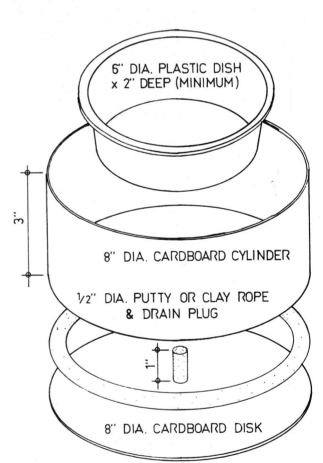

6" DIA. PLASTIC DISH
x 2" DEEP (MINIMUM)

3"

8" DIA. CARDBOARD CYLINDER

½" DIA. PUTTY OR CLAY ROPE
& DRAIN PLUG

1"

8" DIA. CARDBOARD DISK

6"

8"

1. GLUE CARDBOARD CYLINDER TO DISK

2. INSET CLAY OR PUTTY DRAIN PLUG &
   MOLD "ROPE" AROUND THE PERIMETER
   TO FORM THE RECESSED BASE

3. COAT ALL SURFACES WITH LIQUID SOAP
   OR WITH SILICONE MOLD-RELEASE AGENT

4. POUR 1" OF CONCRETE TO FORM THE
   BOTTOM, CENTER THE COATED PLASTIC
   DISH, & POUR THE SIDES

5. CURE THE CONCRETE & REMOVE THE
   FORMS WHEN SET

NOTE: THE CONCRETE MAY BE INTEGRALLY
      COLORED & THE SURFACE MAY BE
      BRUSHED TO EXPOSE THE AGGRE-
      GATE OR PRODUCE A TEXTURE

This simple bonsai dish is handsome and an ideal container for small plants. Note the bonsai saucer. (Photo by Matthew Barr.)

salvage stores or flea markets. Look for dishes (at least 5 or 6 inches deep) with unique outside decoration and handsome glazes. Green or blue colors are particularly handsome, and a footed dish is generally more attractive than one which rests directly on a surface.

Dish Garden Containers

Charming tiny landscapes in dishes are always welcome indoors. Any dish or bowl or pan that is at least 3 inches deep can be put into service. You can use the commercial or homemade bonsai containers for dish gardens, or even metal pans placed in wicker bread baskets for a distinctive arrangement! (If you use aluminum bread or cake pans, set them into the basket-type cover-ups mentioned in Chapter 11.) Small pottery bowls—any kitchen items you have around—can also be used as containers for these tiny gardens. Use simple yet handsome pieces to set off the garden properly.

Because dishes and bowls and pans will not have drainage holes, prepare the soil bed carefully. Put small shards (pieces of broken clay pots) at the bottom of the dish or bowl or pan. Then scatter in gravel chips; the chips will absorb any excess moisture that may accumulate at the bottom of the container. To prevent the soil from turning sour, add a handful of charcoal chips. Then add the soil for the plants.

Teacups   I have seen small plants in delicate teacups at flower shows, and the effect is charming. Use a teacup with a pretty pattern, and plant just one or two tiny plants. As time goes by, trim and prune the plants into nice-looking shapes.

Teacup gardens rely on simplicity and elegance for their beauty, so feature a special plant—perhaps the lovely Spanish shawl, with its tiny leaves and lavender blooms; or the delicate petitpoint ivy. Do not use large-leaved plants because they will be out of place in the teacup. Plant this garden as you would the dish-garden arrangement, using less shards, gravel, and charcoal of course.

A small terra-cotta pot can also be used as a bonsai or dish garden container. (Photo by Joyce R. Wilson.)

This homemade concrete container is quite beautiful and accommodates several succulent plants. (Photo by Joyce R. Wilson.)

Teacup gardens are always charming; this one contains a strawberry geranium. (Photo by Joyce R. Wilson.)

10. Plant Stands, Platforms, Trolleys, Etc.

Years ago potted plants were displayed only on windowsills. Today plants are also featured on plant stands and platforms and trolleys of various designs.

Besides making plants look attractive and decorative, a stand or platform helps your green gems *grow* better; many are designed so that air reaches plant roots and virtually eliminate water stains on carpets or floors – by use of a drip pan (see Drawing 30).

The elevated *stand*, which is actually a pedestal, is a display piece that varies in height from 12 to 36 inches and can hold one or several plants. On the other hand, the plant *platform* is usually 2 to 10 inches high, holds one (maybe two) plants, and is used more for floor or carpet protection than for display. There are some expensive commercial plant stands available, but no commercial plant platforms. However, making your own pieces—either stands or platforms—is inexpensive and actually fun. Plus, by building your own "furniture," you get *exactly* what you want in terms of design, height, material, and finish.

There are many variations of the plant stand and platform; what you make depends entirely on how much money you want to spend and how handy you are with tools. But even the most simple stand or platform will add flair and dimension to a room.

Stands
The single plant stand is usually a pedestal—almost a small, high table. The stand can be round, square, rectangular—almost any shape—and is generally made of wood, mirrored tile, or acrylic. A wooden stand can be as simple as five pieces of plywood cemented together. You can turn the simple wood cube or rectangle into a sophisticated display piece by cementing mirrored tiles onto the wood (variations can be created by using mylar, brass tiles, or reflective contact paper). A basic acrylic plant stand consists of a 10-inch-high cylinder (sold at plastic suppliers) with a circular top glued in place. (Working with acrylic is covered in Chapter 4.) Group several plant stands together and create a planting island, or use stands singly.

Making your own plant stand involves some thought and planning. Keep the design for the stand simple but handsome and of a size that will fit its location. For example, a tall (up to 60 inches) stand is good in a room corner; a 36-inch-high stand is suitable near a window. Wood stands can be left natural or painted to match the decor of the room. In any case, all interior wood plant stands should be built with kiln-dried redwood; outdoor plant stands can be made from construction-grade lumber—a few knots or blemishes are scarcely noticeable outdoors.

There are commercially made plant stands that hold several plants. These have five or six "arms" that hold plants on small trays. Also on the market are tension-pole stands equipped with trays. You can make your own inexpensive multi-plant stand from an acrylic tube or iron pipe fitted with supports and trays.

Other manufactured plant stands are the small, circular tables made of pine and stained and "distressed"; the mahogany tables topped with marble (a Victorian look that is perfect for ferns); and the white, grilled, iron tables for outdoor (or indoor) display.

Metal plant stands may be bought at garden suppliers. In this one several small potted plants have been set. (Photo by Matthew Barr.)

Wood Stand

Drawing 28

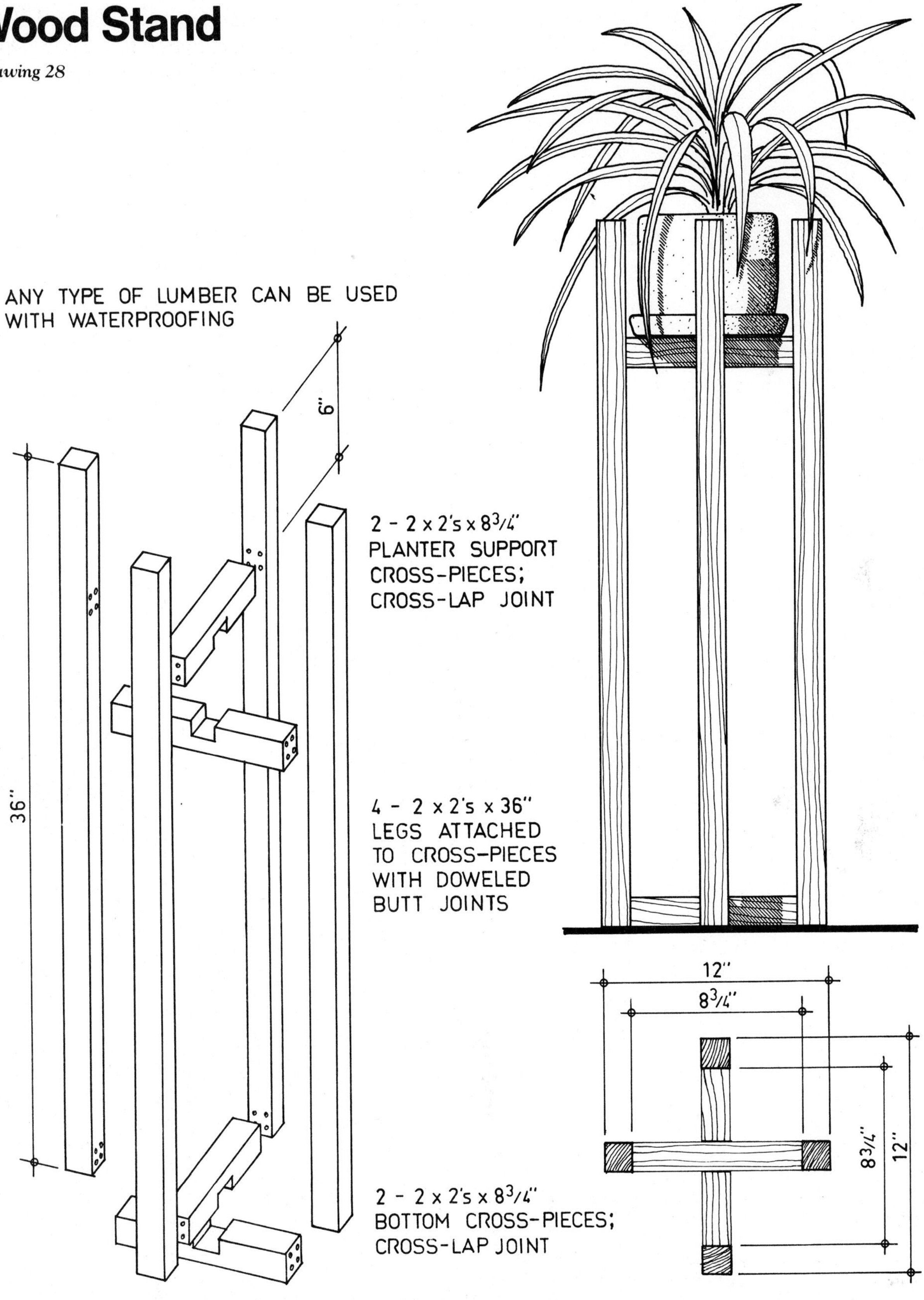

ANY TYPE OF LUMBER CAN BE USED
WITH WATERPROOFING

6"

36"

2 - 2 x 2's x 8$\frac{3}{4}$"
PLANTER SUPPORT
CROSS-PIECES;
CROSS-LAP JOINT

4 - 2 x 2's x 36"
LEGS ATTACHED
TO CROSS-PIECES
WITH DOWELED
BUTT JOINTS

2 - 2 x 2's x 8$\frac{3}{4}$"
BOTTOM CROSS-PIECES;
CROSS-LAP JOINT

12"

8$\frac{3}{4}$"

8$\frac{3}{4}$"

12"

This plant stand, or pedestal, is wood and holds a lovely fern. (Photo courtesy McGuire Furniture Co.)

Platforms   Plants set directly on floors or on dining or end tables and the like invariably present two problems: they are difficult to see, and they usually stain surfaces. But the small platform puts the plant in an enviable viewing position and eliminates any water stains on surfaces. A simple but good-looking platform is a topless acrylic box, 10 inches long by 8 inches wide by 2 inches deep, covered with redwood slats. Put gravel into the box to catch excess water.

Wood-box platforms are equally handsome and easy to build. The top should have holes to hold the pots in place. Or the top can be of wood slats spaced ¼ inch apart (the slats need not be nailed) to hold plants. Put gravel or sphagnum in the box to catch excess water.

You can make circular platforms, too, from acrylic or wooden rounds. And bench-type platforms are also easy to make and cost little.

Trolleys   Don't let the name fool you—plant trolleys are wood platforms with wheels (and are sometimes called dollies). These movable "stages" offer a fine way to move heavy plants around, or any plant for that matter. The unit also raises the plant off floor level—into a better, elevated position—and affords protection from water stains for your floors.

In Drawing 29 we show two typical plant trolleys; one is square, the other round. To add more flair and elegance, we have used several pieces of wood to assemble the unit; but you can also make very simple plant trolleys with a solid block of wood. The main consideration is attaching the casters and this is shown in detail in the drawing.

A highly decorative plant stand enhances the beauty of this bedroom. (Photo by Matthew Barr.)

Plant Trolleys

Drawing 29

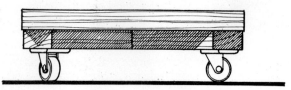

PIECES ARE NAILED INTO SQUARES FIRST,
THEN ONTO THE CROSSPIECE SUPPORT

ALL LUMBER IS
REDWOOD

2"x 4"

2"x 2"

2"x 4"

MITERED CORNERS

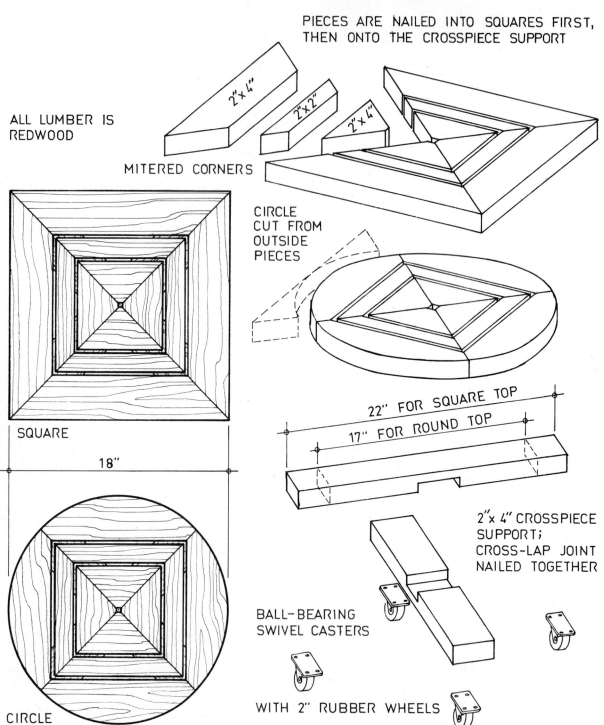

CIRCLE
CUT FROM
OUTSIDE
PIECES

SQUARE

18"

CIRCLE

22" FOR SQUARE TOP

17" FOR ROUND TOP

2"x 4" CROSSPIECE
SUPPORT;
CROSS-LAP JOINT
NAILED TOGETHER

BALL-BEARING
SWIVEL CASTERS

WITH 2" RUBBER WHEELS

Homemade platforms for plants can be made of redwood, such as these. The slats of the stands are spaced ½ inch apart so that air can reach the plants from beneath. (Photo by Clark Photo.)

Drip Pans

Drawing 30

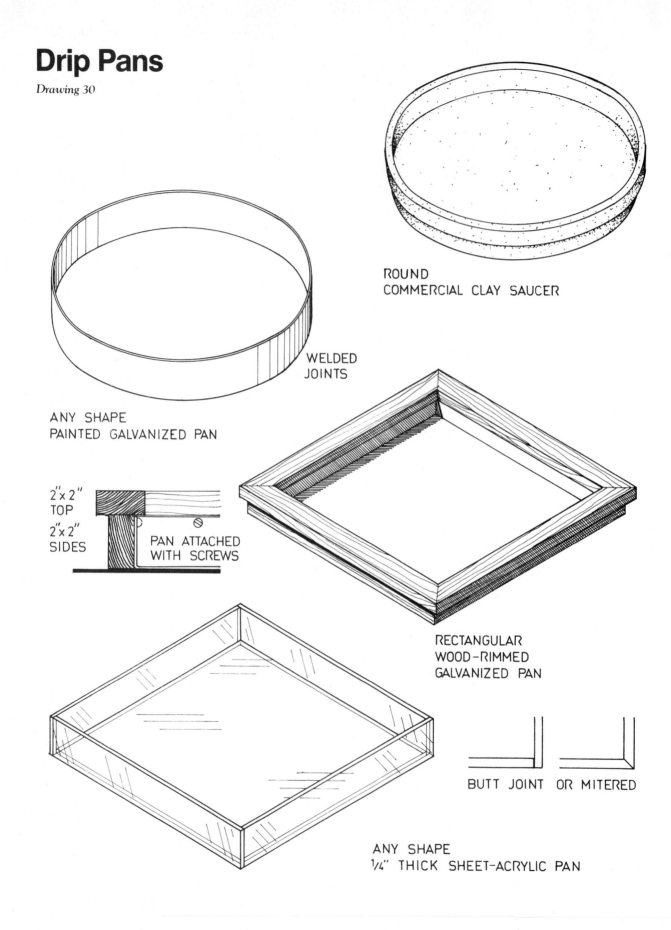

ROUND
COMMERCIAL CLAY SAUCER

WELDED
JOINTS

ANY SHAPE
PAINTED GALVANIZED PAN

2"x 2"
TOP

2"x 2"
SIDES

PAN ATTACHED
WITH SCREWS

RECTANGULAR
WOOD-RIMMED
GALVANIZED PAN

BUTT JOINT OR MITERED

ANY SHAPE
¼" THICK SHEET-ACRYLIC PAN

Tubs with wheels attached are available at nurseries, and these can be used in place of a plant trolley. However, they will cost more than the plant trolley you can make at home.

Variations In addition to wood and acrylic plant stands, platforms, and trolleys, there are other elevated devices you can use and/or make to display your plants. Building supply yards sell inexpensive types of low and handsomely shaped tile or plastic drain pipes that can be used as cylinders to elevate plants. Also consider fruit crates, because some are sturdily and handsomely made. You can modify a fruit crate into a plant stand by adding a plywood side to keep it steady and then adding a coat or two of paint.

Bricks too, as well as cinder blocks, can be arranged into a naturalistic platform. You can use red bricks as they are, or paint them white. Stack two "legs"—each leg of about four or five bricks (or cinder blocks)—and lay a piece of plywood across the legs. Set your plant(s) on the wood.

A wastepaper basket or a cleaned-up giant-size lard can may be painted or covered with paper or burlap and turned upside down. Plants look effective on top of these unusual pedestals.

Brightly painted plastic furniture cubes of varying heights may also be used. But these cubes are expensive, so you might want to think twice about them. (It is really better to make your own plant stands and platforms than to spend unnecessary money.)

Drip Saucers, Pans, and Trays Any container for indoors, whether it is wood, acrylic, clay, or metal, will need a saucer, pan, or tray of some type to catch excess water so that it does not drip on floors or furniture. Standard clay saucers can certainly be used, or try large pie plates. For something more esthetically pleasing, you can have galvanized trays made and then finish them off with wood stripping. (See Drawing 30.) The size of the drip saucer, pan, or tray will of course depend on the size of the container itself.

11. Homemade Cover-ups for Containers

Any decorative container itself can of course be used as a cover-up for a less decorative container such as a clay pot; simply set the pot inside the larger container. But there are, in addition, some fun-producing and unusual ways of inexpensively making your own distinctive *non*-container cover-ups for less attractive containers! Macramé sleeves, for example—which are very handsome.

To make a macramé cover-up for a container, be sure first to cover the container, if it is clay, with foil or plastic before you fit the macramé sleeve or whatever around it—in order to protect the yarn from mold. There are just two basic macramé knots you will need: reverse mounting and double half-hitch knots. With these simple knots you can macramé almost any type of cover-up.

The crocheted cover-up is similar to the macramé sleeve. This cover-up can be done in bold colors. A proficient amateur can make a crocheted holder in an evening. Crochet involves three stitches: the chain, single, and double; all stitches are done with yarn and a crochet hook.

Both hanging wicker and rattan baskets and those set on the floor are modern-looking cover-ups that add warmth and texture to a decor.

Besides using baskets as cover-ups—placing potted plants inside them—it is also possible to waterproof the baskets and plant directly into them (see Drawing 34).

Why not weave your own baskets since the commercial ones are so expensive? By making your own baskets, you can create almost any shape. If you *buy* baskets, you generally are limited to the bow-type or upright ones.

Making Baskets   You can buy rattan or wicker reeds in flat or round shapes, and in several sizes (depending upon the thickness), at hobby stores or upholstery shops. The basic basket consists of circular spokes as the frame, with vertical supporting weavers (see next paragraph). You will also need scissors, a tub of water, a knitting needle or skewer, and a can of clear plastic coating.

To get the reeds flexible, soak them in water for fifteen or more minutes,

MATERIALS

one ball of heavy cord
one large ball of cable cord

MACRAMÉ KNOTS TO USE

Reverse Mounting

Double Half-hitch

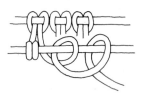

1. Attach twelve lengths of cable cord to the heavy cord, using reverse-mounting knots; you will now have twenty-four lengths of cord from the first round from which to continue.

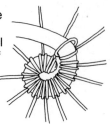

2. Form the second row by tying double half-hitch knots with each knot around the cord.

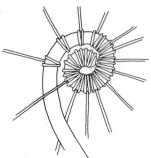

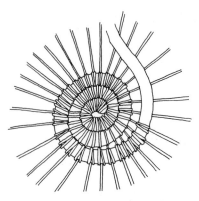

3. Continue as in Step 2, knotting and coiling in an outward spiral.

4. When the spiral is the size of the base of the container, begin the sides by positioning the cable cord slightly above each round.

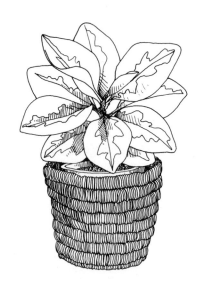

5. When the desired height has been achieved, cut the cable cord and tuck the end into the inside of the macramé cover.

Making a Macramé Cover
Drawing 31

MATERIALS

one skein yarn
crochet hook

STITCHES NEEDED TO MAKE
FIVE GRANNY SQUARES

1. Chain Stitch: Pull the yarn
through the loop on the hook;
insert the hook into the slip knot,
and wrap the yarn around the
hook clockwise.

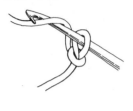

2. Single Stitch: Insert the hook
under the two top loops of the
second chain from the hook; pull
the yarn through on the hook.

3. Double Stitch: Pull the yarn
through the two loops on the
hook.

Ending a Piece:

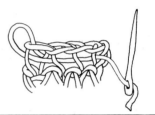

Slip-stitch the squares together at their edges.

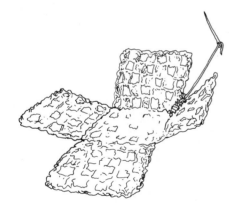

Insert a pot into
the cover.

To make a *hanging* cover, crochet
four 30″ strands, using a chain stitch.

Crocheting a Cover
Drawing 32

depending on the type or thickness of the reeds. If the reeds become rigid while you are weaving, soak the basket-to-be in water for about ten minutes, or until you can again flex the reeds. Use eight or more long spokes and one short spoke. To lash the spokes together use "weavers". These are the reeds woven over and under the spokes. Keep the weavers equidistant so the weaving will be uniform. Weave over and under the spokes—where necessary, use the knitting needle or skewer to keep the spaces open between the spokes. Continue weaving until the base of the basket is the size you want. Then pull the weavers tight and bend the spokes to form the base of the basket.

When the base is finished, place a flower pot on it, and continue weaving loosely around the pot with a round weaver. To insert the flat weaver, weave it around the spokes, leaving a 2-inch tail inside the basket. Then weave the tail into the next row.

This handsome basket holds an orchid and makes a fine cover-up for the pot inside. (Photo by Matthew Barr.)

MATERIALS
ten size #3 spokes, 28″ long
one size #3 spoke, 14″ long
three size #1 weavers
fifteen size #3 weavers
scissors

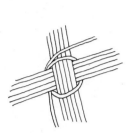 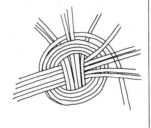

1. Arrange ten long spokes in a cross and make one round with a size #1 weaver.

2. After completing four rounds, begin weaving *under* two and *over* two spokes.

3. Add the odd size #3 spoke to create an alternating pattern from one row to the next; continue weaving under and over, treating the odd spoke as if it were two.

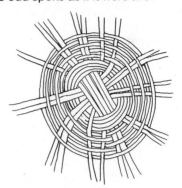

4. When one weaver runs out, overlap a new one (size #1) and continue; the base is completed when all three size #1 weavers have been used.

5. Separate the pairs of spokes in the base to singles, and begin weaving in the size #3 weavers, forming an under-and-over pattern between the spokes.

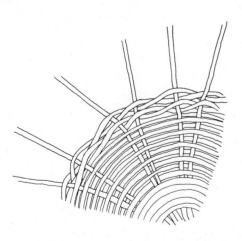

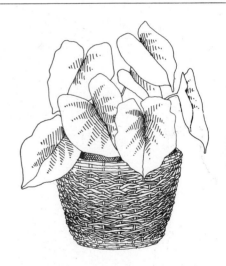

6. Continue weaving and, when desired, weave the top border over two and under two—five times—and finish by clipping off the spoke ends.

Making a Wicker Basket
Drawing 33

Five Helpful Hints   Here are some points to remember:

1. Try to make the base so that it pops up in the center; then the basket will rest on its outer edges.

2. Press the base into a dome shape while weaving it.

3. Keep the distance between the spokes as uniform as possible.

4. Keep the weavers perpendicular to the spokes.

5. When the basket is completed, apply a coat of clear plastic spray to strengthen and protect it.

A sturdy basket without waterproofing will last at least 1 to 2 years. I have some which I bought several years ago that are still in good shape. Waterproofed baskets, with newspaper liners as described below, will last considerably longer.

Baskets can also be made from rushes, grass, and wicker, depending on your expertise with these materials. There are several good books about basket weaving at libraries, if you want to pursue the subject. Most woven baskets are best used as pot cover-ups rather than for direct planting. However, if you do want to use a basket as a planter, be sure to waterproof it, as follows.

Baskets like this fairly simple one are often used as cover-ups for potted plants. (Photo by Matthew Barr.)

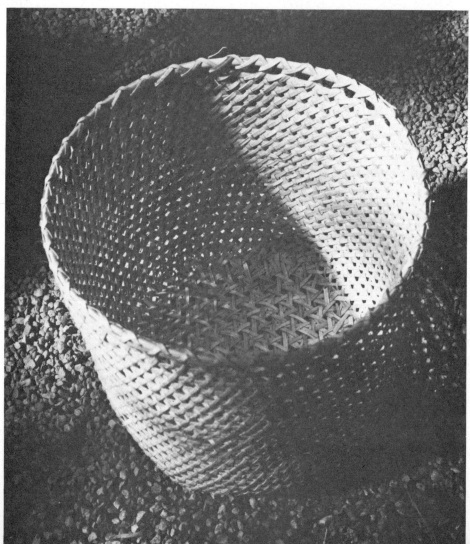

This handwoven basket, suitable as a cover-up for a potted plant, will lend a decorative note to any room. (Photo by Matthew Barr.)

Decals such as the ones on this pot can be used to embellish or "cover up" a plain or unattractive container. Or you can paint designs on the container. (Photo by Matthew Barr.)

MATERIALS

newspaper

clear polyester resin

clear polyester hardener

old tin or plastic bucket, for mixing

gloves

brush

1. Cut or tear the newspaper into long, narrow strips.

2. Following the directions on the cans, mix the resin and hardener; soak the newspaper strips in this mixture.

3. After having brushed the mixture over the inside of the basket to be waterproofed, apply the dripping strips to conform with the shape of the basket's interior.

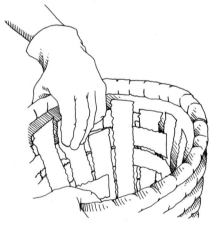

4. Allow the first layer to dry before adding a second (place alternating strips at right angles) and further layers—until you have built up about ten layers of paper.

5. After the final paper-and-resin layering, brush a final coat of the mixture over the inside of the basket for a complete seal. Allow a few days for the resin to dry thoroughly before planting the waterproofed container.

Waterproofing a Basket

Drawing 34

Waterproofing Baskets

I must warn you in advance that waterproofing baskets is a fairly messy and time-consuming process. You will need clear polyester resin and polyester hardener, newspapers, gloves, and a brush.

First, cut or tear the newspaper into long, narrow strips. Next, following the directions on the cans, mix the resin with the hardener. Now brush the mixture all over the inside of the basket to be waterproofed. Use a thin, even coat rather than a splotchy, thick one. Next, dip the newspaper strips in the resin mixture and apply them to the inside of the basket, covering the bottom and sides completely. Allow each layer to dry completely before adding the next layer. Use alternating strips at right angles over the layer below it, creating a crisscross effect. Continue to cover the basket with more layers of resin-soaked newspaper strips, until you have built up about ten layers of paper.

When you have finished the paper-and-resin layering, brush a coat of resin over the entire inside and let the resin harden until there is a complete seal. Test the seal by pouring water into the basket. If there is leakage, let the basket dry and then repeat the paper-and-resin layering.

Whenever you are waterproofing baskets, be sure that you work outside because resin fumes are dangerous to inhale, and always wear gloves when working with resin materials.

Paste-ons

Paste-ons are not container cover-ups in the true sense. What you do is adhere fabric pieces in various shapes—diamonds, squares, whatever—to a simple, plain, or even ugly clay pot with a polymer acrylic paint; in other words, the paste-on "covers up" the less attractive pot. Another good paste-on plan is to glue yarn to a pot. Or you can simply paint your pots white and then add your own delicate designs or initials with a colored paint. Still more paste-ons are strips of colored paper, small seashells, mosaic tiles, beads, seeds, and sequins. The possibilities are almost endless.

How to Work with Paste-ons

No matter which type of paste-on you use, you must first coat the porous clay pot with a clear polyurethane sealer (available at hardware stores). To apply bulky or heavy decorative pieces such as seashells and so forth, use a waterproof glue; if you are using paper paste-ons, simply seal them on with the polyurethane sealer.

Many of the materials needed for these paste-on ideas are sold at hobby stores; and paints and sealers are at hardware stores. There is some minimal expense involved, but you will find paste-ons are a delightful way to add a personal touch to your impersonal clay pots.

12. A Repotting Primer

Putting a plant in a new container is not as simple as some garden writers make it sound. Potting is actually a very critical part of successful plant culture; if the plant gets off to a bad start, it can never really thrive. Potting a small plant in a 7-inch-diameter pot is relatively easy; you do not have too much soil to work with and the container is not awkward to handle. But consider the large plant that goes into a box or tub or planter of over 20 inches length or diameter. You are dealing with a heavy amount of soil and also a hard-to-handle container. Planting in wire baskets (see Drawing 17) or other hanging containers also requires some expertise. This chapter will cover the various facets of potting.

Removing New Plants from Their Containers

By new plants I mean those plants bought from nurseries and already in containers. Most of these plants will be repotted into your new, hopefully *handcrafted* containers. The procedure for removing a plant from its old container depends on whether the container is a metal can, a clay pot, or a plastic pot. The plant should be removed with as little shock as possible.

If the plant you bought is in a can, be sure to have the nursery cut the can along the sides before you take it home. Cutting cans on your own involves buying an expensive can cutter. Once you have the can slit on both sides by the nursery people, you will have to repot the plant that day. Waiting can severely damage the plant because the roots will dry out.

When you get the plant home, put the canned plant on a level surface—I use the ground—and put one foot on the edge of the can to hold it in place. Then grasp the collar, or base, of the plant with your hands and gently pull and tease the plant from the can. If the plant does not come out, put the can on its side and again hold it down with one foot while trying the pull-and-tease method.

Removing a plant from a clay, plastic, or Styrofoam container is usually easier than taking one from a can. If the plant is medium-sized, lift the container up and hit the sides of the pot against an old table or sink to loosen the plant. Then grasp the collar of the plant and ease it from the housing. Occasionally a plant has been in a clay pot so long that it just will not budge. If so, run a knife carefully all around the inside surface of the pot; if that doesn't work, crack the pot with a hammer. It is better to lose the old pot—which is usually soiled anyway—than to harm the plant by tugging and pulling.

Once the plant is out of its original container, crumble away the old, loose soil. Bear in mind that you want to keep as much of the original soil around the *roots* as possible—this is called keeping the root ball intact—but you want to remove some of it. Trim away the brown-edged roots but do not disturb the others. The plant is now ready for its new container.

Potting
To pot in any small- to medium-sized container—up to 10 inches in diameter—fill the bottom of the container with a 1-inch layer of pot shards (pieces of old pots). For larger containers use 2 inches of shards. Scatter some charcoal chips on the shards (charcoal keeps the soil sweet), and then put in a mound of soil. Scatter some perlite around the mound to help keep the soil open. Position the plant. If the plant is too high in the pot or tub, remove some soil; if the plant is too low, add soil. When the plant is positioned properly, fill in and around it with new soil. Pack the soil down around the plant with more fresh soil. To eliminate air pockets, pack down the soil with your thumbs or a potting stick; but do not pack it in too tightly—you want the soil to remain porous. That is, you want the soil to have air spaces in it.

When the plant is in its container—and allow ½ to 1 inch unfilled space at the top of the container for watering—apply water slowly and thoroughly to the soil. Be sure that excess water drains from the container. Then water the plant again, so the soil is thoroughly moist.

All containers should be clean, so scrub any old ones you use. Soak new clay containers with water so that they do not absorb the water the plant needs when you pot it.

Repotting
Eventually, in a year or so, you should remove a plant from its container because the plant will have outgrown its old home. More importantly, the soil has been depleted of its nutrients, and fresh soil is needed.

Small containers should present few, if any, problems, but with large containers it is not easy to get the plant out of the soil. Lifting a 24-inch box is out of the question; therefore, first you have to dig out the soil. With a blunt-edged stick or hand trowel, remove the surface soil to a depth of about 6 to 8 inches if you are working with a 20- or 24-inch container. Keep digging out the soil until you can wiggle the plant with your hands. Then use the pull-and-tease method to get the plant out. If the plant still will not come out easily, keep digging away soil. This is work, but it is the only method of harmlessly getting the plant out *and* saving the container.

I have chosen to end this book with repotting information, but this chapter could just as well have been the opener to the book. In either case it makes little difference; the important thing is that you do repot plants, as necessary, so they can grow well for you. New soil gives them new vigor. And of course new containers—those you make yourself—for your own plants give you and the plant a lift. There is great satisfaction in growing a plant well, and equal joy in creating a container especially for a favorite plant!